'The Fairest Arch in England'

Old Ouse Bridge, York, and its Buildings: The Pictorial Evidence

By Barbara Wilson and Frances Mee

Published by the York Archaeological Trust   2002

The next day, being Wednesday the 13th July [1664], they went to the famous cittie of Yorke ...
thorow the cittie runneth the river Ouse, in which bridge is the fairest arch in England.

(Robert Davies (ed.), 1863, *The Life of Marmaduke Rawdon of York,*
Camden Society **85**, 116)

T

Contents

List of Figures

Introduction

This is the second fascicule in *The Archaeology of York* Supplementary Series which deals with the pictorial evidence for the medieval buildings of York. Its main topic is 'Old' Ouse Bridge, built in 1565 and taken down in 1810–18, when it was replaced by the present structure. There is very little archaeological evidence available for a study of the bridge. All that remain visible today are a few stones on the King's Staith and fragments of carved masonry from the bridge chapel in the Yorkshire Museum, the rest of the stonework having gone to provide infill for the new bridge or for building work along the nearby waterfronts. Documentary and pictorial evidence are therefore of paramount importance, and York is fortunate in possessing excellent collections of both.

The Tudor bridge with its large and unusual central arch, crowned by its bridge chapel, council chamber, shops and houses, and framed by the river and its waterfronts, drew admiring, indeed effusive, comments from visitors and attracted artists of both local and national importance. The imminent demise of the bridge from c.1800 encouraged local artists, notably Joseph Halfpenny and Henry Cave, to produce drawings and prints which aimed to give an accurate record of the structure before it was lost. Naturally, visiting artists, such as Turner, Girtin, Farington and Cotman, were less concerned with accuracy than with artistic vision. Examples of both attitudes have been included in this volume. Most artists experienced some difficulty in depicting the shape of the central arch and argued whether it was pointed or semicircular (in fact, it was neither, see pp.57–8), and again examples have been given here to illustrate this.

In order to place the bridge in its historical context, brief descriptions of its Roman and medieval predecessors and its successor, the present Ouse Bridge, have been included as well as an essay on bridge-building in general. Topographical context is provided by a short introductory outline of the importance of the River Ouse and its water-borne traffic, and a birds'-eye view of the medieval and post-medieval waterfronts. As in the first fascicule, these essays are merely introductory guidelines, to be followed up by the interested reader or specialist researcher. Only brief reference is made to other bridges over the Ouse in York, not least because they are not medieval.

The guide to illustrative material is in the form of a gazetteer. Illustrations are listed chronologically by topic, with date, title, artist, medium, location and reference number of the original, together with any explanatory notes. Illustration numbers are cited at the start of each figure caption. We have not listed all possible views, much less illustrated them: the bridge and river were hugely popular with artists of very varied attainment; many pictures were merely copies, and, frankly, over-exposure to views of marked similarity can become wearisome. For general information on 19th-century topographical illustration and the variety of techniques used by artists, see *AY* Supplementary Series: Wilson and Mee 1998, 19–22.

A final note about orientation. The Ouse flows generally south-east, but forms an S-bend at Clifton before turning south-east again, then gradually south as it leaves the city at Clementhorpe and Fulford. To avoid confusion, we have here referred merely to the east (or left) bank and west (or right) bank.

Acknowledgements

The authors owe a huge debt of gratitude to many individuals and organisations: to Dominic Tweddle without whose inspiration the project would never have got off the ground; to York Archaeological Trust's Board of Trustees for their support; to David Stocker for his valuable suggestions and help with the architectural aspects of St William's Chapel; to David Palliser, Richard Hall and Nigel Tringham who all read and commented on the text at various stages; to Valerie Black for access to notes and other material produced by the late David Black; to those people who have helped so willingly with picture research and supplying illustrations (Victoria Osborne formerly of York City Art Gallery, now of the City of Birmingham Art Gallery; Allison Sharpe of York City Art Gallery; Amanda Howard and other staff at York Reference Library; Antonino Vella of Wakefield Museums and Arts; staff at the Borthwick Institute of Historical Research; Louise Hampson and other staff at York Minster Archives; Elizabeth Hartley, Mel Cook and Melanie Baldwin of the Yorkshire Museum; Timothy Goodhue and Melissa Gold of the Yale Center for British Art; Louise Bythell and Adrian Gibbs of the Bridgeman Art Library; Nick Wharton, Civic Secretary at The Mansion House, York; staff at Leeds District Archives; staff at the Tate Gallery; staff at the British Museum, Department of Prints and Drawings; Linda Fowler, Collections Administrator at Eton College, Windsor; Brett Dolman, Curator of the Manuscripts Collection, British Library; Syd Heppell, Keeper of the Evelyn Collection; Alyson Rogers of the National Monuments Records Centre).

In addition, there are many individuals whose help has been given in many different ways and to whom the authors wish to express their gratitude: Glenys Boyles, Paul Chesmore (York Millennium Bridge Trust Limited), Simon Chew, Lesley Collett, Anthony Crawshaw, Barrie Dobson, Paul Harvey, Simon Hill, Kevin Leahy (North Lincolnshire Museum, Scunthorpe), Denis Moor, Patrick Ottaway, William K. Sessions, John C. Taylor, Ian Travers.

The publication could not have come to fruition without the financial support of the following institutions, to which the authors and York Archaeological Trust would like to express their thanks: the Council for British Archaeology; the Friends of York Archaeological Trust; the Marc Fitch Fund; the Scouloudi Foundation in association with the Institute of Historical Research; the Sheldon Memorial Trust; York Common Good Trust; Yorkshire Archaeological Society; Yorkshire Architectural and York Archaeological Society.

The illustrations are reproduced by courtesy of York Museums Trust, York Art Gallery (Figs.8–9, 14, 19–21, 37, 46, 49–50, 54–7, 59–60, 62–3, 68–9, 71, 74–5), York Reference Library (Figs.4, 6, 10–11, 36, 47, 61, 64, 70), Wakefield Museums and Arts (Fig.35), the Borthwick Institute of Historical Research (Fig.51), York Minster, © Dean and Chapter of York (back cover), the Yorkshire Museum, © Yorkshire Museum (Figs.18, 32–4), the Yale Center for British Art and the Bridgeman Art Library (Figs.58 and 67), City of York Council, Mansion House (Figs.19, 45, 63, 71), the British Museum (Figs.23 and 38), the Tate Gallery (Figs.53 and 66), English Heritage, © Crown copyright, NMR (Fig.31), the Evelyn Collection (Figs.43 and 77). Figs.44–5 and 52 were photographed by Simon I. Hill (Scirebröc). Figs.54–5, 76 are from the collection of the late David Black, reproduced by kind permission of Valerie Black. Figs.15–17 were drawn by Simon Chew.

2

The Setting
The River Ouse

'The River Ouse, that mud-stained torrent, which owns neither mouth nor source, has always played a prominent part in the country's history.' This is how Tom Bradley opened his essay on the Ouse in 1891. It has also been described as the 'First Cause' of the City of York, and as a 'Constant', along with the Minster, in its history (Knight 1944, 35, 65). While discoveries of scattered prehistoric artefacts indicate pre-Roman settlement, temporary or permanent but undoubtedly small in scale, the history of the city begins with the foundation of a Roman fortress in or about AD 71. The confluence of the Ouse and Foss provided both a measure of natural defence and a means of communication by water with Lincoln, southern Britain and the Continent. The fortress was designed to take advantage of this strategic position, and laid out a street pattern that largely determined the topographical development of modern York. Over succeeding centuries the river provided a food and water supply, and, most importantly, the means by which York became one of the great medieval trading cities of the country, before contributing finally to leisure and tourism.

During the Roman occupation, the river added an extra means of defence to the fortress, but only for as long as it also had walls and a garrison. Once the garrison was removed and the walls fell into disrepair, the Ouse provided a means of entry for Anglian and Anglo-Scandinavian invaders; by the 11th century the Norman castle existed to protect the river rather than being protected by it.

To York citizens the river was most important as a means of trade and communication, linking the city to the coast by way of the Humber and, for smaller boats, to the south and west by way of its tributaries. Until 1757 the Ouse was tidal as far as 'popleton fferry wch is about 4 miles above ye Citty . . . [and] . . . upon extraordinary Tides it ever flowed Higher' (Trinity House Report 1698, quoted in Duckham 1967, 17). Navigators could make use of the rapid flood tide to travel upstream, though they might have to resort to towing on occasion (Fig.1). The slower ebb tide, however, was insufficient to scour the silt from the river bed, leaving shoals which needed careful navigation. The presence of a river-pilot in Roman

Fig.1 (no.4) *The view north from just below the confluence of the Ouse and Foss, in the Fishergate area. St George's Field is in the centre, between the two rivers; the Castle, Castle Mills and the Minster can be seen in the background. The small turret on the south-west angle of the Minster tower was erected for signalling and observation by order of the 2nd Duke of Buckingham in 1666 and was removed in 1808, so pictorial views can be dated by it (Butler 1978, 35). A good-size, two-masted sailing ship is portrayed in the foreground and a laden barge is being towed upstream — there is certainly a rope attached to its mast and a man on the bank is holding the rope. A towpath can be seen on the left, and both rivers have sandy banks on the right as viewed from this point.*

Fig.2 *(no.7) View looking upstream towards Ouse Bridge from Clementhorpe in 1736, with the Minster and Castle in the background. It gives an indication of the open space on either side of the river; the limes and elders of the New Walk were a recent addition, having been planted in 1731–2. The boats which are keeling over at the King's Staith near the bridge may indicate the shallowness of the river at low tide; alternatively it may be that boats were unloaded from one side and then from the other, the weight distribution causing the vessel to list. There are other sailing boats and smaller rowing boats on the river.*

York reflects the importance of this (*AY* 1, 104; Ottaway 1993, fig.21). In addition to the tides, boatmen had to contend with the natural and often rapid rise and fall resulting from flooding or drought whereby boats could be stranded at their moorings, as may be suggested by the ships shown keeling over at the King's Staith in Fig.2.

Little is known of the commercial use made of the river in Roman York, but it is reasonable to assume river transport for heavy or bulky goods such as stone from Tadcaster brought via the Wharfe; sherds of pottery such as amphorae, containers for olive oil and wine, indicate imports from the Continent. Excavation within the cellars of 39–41 Coney Street during 1974–5 (YAT site code 1974–5.18) uncovered what have been

interpreted as timber storage sheds or warehouses for grain, linked with the provisioning of the military garrison in its early years at York. This grain may have been imported from the south-east of England, making use of the River Ouse (*AY* 14/2; *AY* 6/1, 16–18). Structural remains have been excavated near the Foss, all convenient for access to the south-east gate of the fortress (RCHMY **1**, 64–5), and it is likely that the Roman civilian settlement was served by wharves on the Ouse near the present North Street and Skeldergate. Indeed, a grain store on the *colonia* bank of the river was located at 5 Rougier Street in 1981–2 (*AY* 6/1, 19).

There was little archaeological evidence for overseas trade in the Anglian period until excavation of the Fishergate area by York Archaeological Trust in the 1980s revealed a settlement, possibly part of an extensive trading *wic* in the 7th to 9th centuries (*AY* 7/1). It has been suggested as the site of the colony of Frisian merchants referred to by Altfrid (*AY* 1, 131–2). There is much evidence for commercial activity in Anglo-Scandinavian York: small finds include coins and merchants' scales for weighing silver, together with imported goods and raw materials such as cloth from Germany and the Low Countries, amber from the Baltic, and silk and dyestuffs from the Eastern Mediterranean reaching York by way of Scandinavian ports and possibly other markets in England. This evidence lends support to the enthusiastic contemporary comment that the city was 'enriched with the treasures of merchants, who come from all parts, but above all from the Danish people' in that it indicates the extent of trade; the volume of trade and the use of the river and its frontages are, as yet, more difficult to deduce (Hall 1994, 83–8; *AY* 1, 171–2; see pp.10–21 for the waterfronts).

Much of the commercial area at the confluence of the Ouse and Foss rivers was destroyed by the building of the Norman castle which, with its counterpart across the Ouse, was designed as a defence against river-borne invaders. In the longer term, however, the demands of military and ecclesiastical building increased the river traffic, as stone was shipped by way of the Wharfe and the Ouse, roofing lead came downstream from Boroughbridge and much of the glass came by river from the Continent. Over the succeeding centuries, York merchants came to dominate the region's trade, exporting wool (later replaced by cloth) and lead to the Netherlands, Germany and the Baltic, along with smaller amounts of farm produce such as hides and butter. A wide variety of goods was imported including flax, iron, timber and pitch from the Baltic; dyestuffs, spices, prunes, currants and the occasional 'oliphant's tethe' from the entrepôt ports of Holland; wine from Bordeaux; figs, wine, oranges and lemons from Spain. Among the luxury goods imported for redistribution to wealthy northern landowners were consignments of velvet, Spanish silk, Venetian gold and 'estridge wool'. The coastal trade included salt, fish and, increasingly, coal from Newcastle, and utensils, haberdashery and groceries from London.

York's prosperity reached its peak at the end of the 14th century, and decline becomes evident from c.1450, as cloth manufacture moved to the West Riding and as the increase in the size of sea-going vessels necessitated trans-shipment of goods in Hull, increasing the cost of transport. There was some resurgence in the late 16th century, and some overseas merchants could still make a good living, but a serious trade depression developed in the 1620s: a certificate of shipping owned by York men in 1626 lists only nine ships, ranging from 20 to 60 tons apiece, and 29 sailors (*YCHB* **35**, fo.21). Many factors impeded York's trade, among them foreign wars, piracy and, above all, Dutch competition, but little could be done about these. Instead the corporation attempted to improve river navigation, first by the removal of fish garths and the clearance of silt and shoals, then by a more ambitious scheme to shorten the 63 miles to Hull by means of a cut. Such a scheme needed technical expertise, considerable financial outlay and powerful backing. In 1616 John Hart, armed with a map of the proposed cut (Fig.3), was sent to Holland to find a suitably skilled man; he returned with three men and a claim for expenses that only exacerbated the financial problem. Endeavours to get the support of James I on his visits to York in 1603 and 1617 produced promises but no action. Meanwhile the city's MPs were instructed to seek an act of parliament to facilitate the scheme, but their letters reveal only increasing frustration as king and parliamentary leaders quarrelled over finance and the constitution; local matters were pushed aside, to be lost entirely as one parliament after another was brought to a premature end (*YCHB* **34**, fos.219v, 221). In 1657 an act was procured, but this only lasted for twelve months and in 1659 it was agreed that its execution should be suspended. Again politics intervened and nothing was done until in 1727 an act was passed empowering a body of trustees to make improvements and levy tolls (Wilson 1967, 139–43). The creation of Naburn lock in 1757 allowed the passage of larger boats, but by now the only wholesale trade was in butter, brought to the market in Mickle-gate and sent downriver from Topham's Staith. Though this was mainly in the hands of London merchants, it did encourage some boat building until it was brought to an end largely by Irish competition. Local transport of heavy or bulky goods such as coal, newsprint and basic foodstuffs continued by barge, and in the 19th century there were regular passenger services by steamboat to Selby and Hull, until the coming of the railway provided York with swifter and more reliable services after 1840. A century after the opening of Naburn lock its capacity was proving

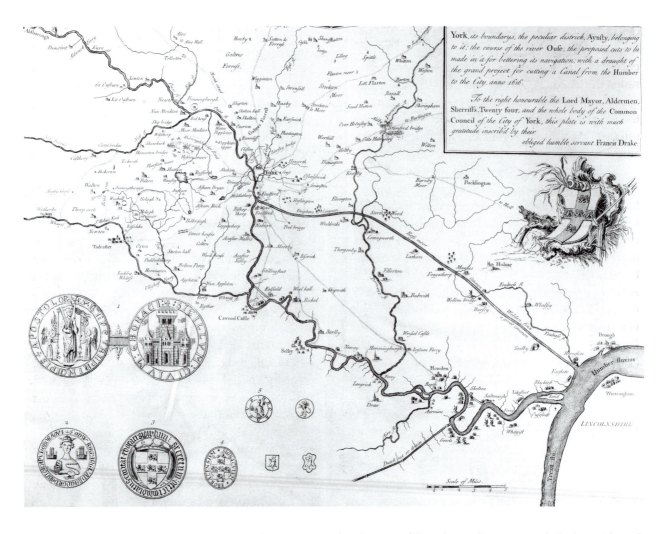

Fig.3 *(no.6) Proposed canal from the Humber to the Ouse, 1616. The River Ouse followed a winding course and silted up with sand, so it was decided to cut a canal starting at Fulford on the Ouse and finishing at Broomfield near Brough on the Humber. It seems that smaller cuts may also have been planned, to get rid of bends in the river, for example, one at Cawood and another on the Humber side of Selby.*

insufficient and in 1888 a new lock was opened, alongside the old one. Vessels of up to 400 tons could now pass through to York.

Boat building and repair work took place at Skeldergate from the 17th century at least. Francis Place's view from Clifford's Tower c.1706 shows a half-built boat on the river bank opposite St George's Field (no.5) and Nathaniel Whittock's bird's-eye view of 1858 shows a boatyard just south of Lendal Tower on the east bank of the river (Fig.8, p.12). The vessels constructed were in the main fairly small, such as keels and sloops. The Humber keel was the local maid-of-all-work, capable of carrying cargoes far inland from the Humber ports to the many towns and villages on the rivers and connecting inland water-

ways. The keel has been recorded as a distinct class of vessel in Yorkshire since the medieval period but it bears some similarities to Viking trading craft, particularly the hull shape and square sail (Ellis 1982, 33). The Humber keel carries a single mast on which are set a square mainsail and topsail. It was very strongly built of oak, had extremely bluff bows, rounded stern and flat bottom. Some were clinker-built and early Fox Talbot photographs of the Ouse in the 1840s show small clinker-built keels. Keels were in regular use on the Ouse in York, carrying coal, grain, foodstuffs and agricultural produce. Boats shown in some of the pictures reproduced here (e.g. Figs.39, 67) may well be Humber keels, but the masts have been lowered in many of them so it is impossible to tell if the sails were square. The single mast of a keel was approximately one-third of the vessel's length from the bow. This is one of the main differences from the Humber sloop, another vessel which sailed the Ouse, whose mast was set further forward, approximately one-fifth of the vessel's length from the stern. The sloop had a large fore-and-aft mainsail on a long boom extending aft to the steering position. It may be seen in Figs.1, 67 and 68.

Shipbuilding beyond Skeldergate Postern seems to have reached a peak at the end of the 18th century. Between 1769 and 1771 six brigantines were constructed, one named the 'Ouse', with a capacity of 80–100 tons; they were used largely for the butter trade between York and London (Taylor 1990, 31–2). A further three large brigantines were constructed in 1776–7, and three more in the 100-ton range (the upper limit imposed by the dimensions of the first Naburn lock) were built in 1781, 1783 and 1797 (Taylor 1992, 25). A true brigantine is a two-masted vessel with a square-rigged fore-mast and a fore-and-aft rigged main-mast with square sails on the top-mast. The term is often used less precisely to describe such a vessel without the square sails on the main-mast.

Some artists seem to have taken great care to draw or paint vessels on the Ouse accurately and to scale, for example, Halfpenny (Fig.39), White (Fig.42), Girtin (Fig.67) and Taylor (Fig.68). Others, notably Toms (Fig.40), have drawn ships (vessels with three or more masts and fully square-rigged) which probably never sailed through York and would not have

been able to pass beneath the central arch of Ouse Bridge. Many smaller vessels would have been in daily use on the Ouse in York, mainly rowing boats (see Figs.9, 37 and 46), small sailing boats (see Figs.58 and 61) and ferries (see Figs.4 and 9).

In the days when there was only one bridge crossing the Ouse in York, there were two ferry crossings in the city centre. From medieval times a ferry plied between Lendal Tower on the north bank and Barker Tower at the North Street Postern (Fig.9, p.14). The Bridgemasters' Accounts between 1428 and 1446 record 'And for John Sharpp, ferryman, for a licence granted to him for ferrying across the Use between Seynt Lenardlendyng and Barkerlendyng . . . this year 40s.' (YCA/C82:3, C82:5, C82:7, C82:11, C82:12; AY 2/2). Later, in the 1450s, the Accounts record 'And for the farm of the ferry-toll across the Ouse there in the tenure of John Coupland . . . 28s. 6d.' (YCA/83:2, C83:4, C83:5, C83:7; ibid.). It seems that from the 15th century Lendal ferry was let by the city corporation to the highest bidder. In June 1477, for example, the York House Book records:

John Newton appeared before the mayor John Tong, the chamberlains, and other men of the city, and leased the ferry across the River Ouse at Saint Leonard's landing, with each and every of its wages, fees, profits and advantages belonging to it, from last Pentecost for a term of twenty years. No other person will be allowed a ferry from the city during that time, except for his own use or that of his household. Newton will pay five marks annually for

Fig.4 (no.52c) In this drawing Lendal ferry is being pulled in and tied off on the North Street side of the river, and a lady is waiting to board it. The Guildhall and river frontage are well depicted.

rent of the ferry, the first payment to be made next Martinmas (Attreed 1991, 88–9).

This ferry features prominently in Gastineau's 1826 watercolour view of the Ouse (no.22), and the ferry boat is being tied up in Ridsdale Tate's tracing of J. Browne's ink wash drawing of North Street Postern and Lendal ferry (Fig.4). By the 19th century, however, it was obvious that York, with its rapidly increasing population, badly needed another bridge crossing. In 1862, the last year Lendal ferry operated, the ferryman John Leeman carried 293,460 passengers, over 800 a day. The cast iron Lendal Bridge, designed by Thomas Page and sited at the old ferry crossing because of the location of York's railway station, was opened in January 1863.

York's other ferry crossing, shown on Nathaniel Whittock's bird's-eye view of the city (Fig.8), was at Skeldergate (see also Fig.14, p.20). In July 1541 the city corporation agreed 'there shal be a bote and a common ferye beneyth the common crayn and the said watter bailey to have the profit therof' (Murray 1988, 28). The 'common crane', which loaded and unloaded the goods of all merchants apart from freemen of York, was positioned on the south bank of the Ouse just inside the city walls beside Skeldergate Postern. By the beginning of the 19th century the ferry was leased by the corporation to a person 'whose duty it is to be in constant attendance during the day' and who charged a halfpenny for every passenger carried (ibid.). The expansion of the south-eastern part of the city during the 19th century made it imperative that the Skeldergate ferry be replaced with a bridge. A survey in 1874 showed that 73,560 people had crossed the river in the ferry boat in the previous three months, an average of 809 a day. Skeldergate Bridge finally opened in 1881, a five-arched bridge designed by George Page, son of the designer of Lendal Bridge.

Until the opening of Selby bridge in 1792 York's Ouse Bridge was the only crossing on the entire length of the river down to the sea. Consequently ferries were vital to the daily life of people living either side of the river. In the immediate vicinity of York alone there were ferry crossings at Poppleton, Clifton, Bishopthorpe, Naburn and Acaster Selby (see Fig.5).

Alcuin's description of the Ouse as 'piscosa' (teeming with fish) is a further reminder of its importance to the Roman and medieval economy (*AY* 1, 129–30). Analysis of fish-bones from early medieval deposits in Fishergate and Coppergate revealed salmon, pike, eel and coarse fish. Stocks of some varieties declined after the 10th century, an indication of water pollution resulting from the growth of the city. Salmon, cheap in York even by medieval standards, continued to flourish in the Ouse into the 20th century, though by the 12th century sea fish were replacing pike and salmon in popularity. There is documentary evidence for other fish, though this often means that they were a rarity, such as the sturgeon measuring 'two yards a half and an ynche' presented to the corporation in 1601. Much of the fishing was done by means of fish garths, enclosures of timber and wicker, probably with nets, set transversely across the river and divided into 'rowmes' or compartments. By their nature they left little archaeological evidence, and there is a marked lack of contemporary illustration or description. In essence they probably resembled those that can still be seen in many places, such as the Solway Firth in Scotland and Toome Bridge in Northern Ireland (though these are eel traps). A survey of 1484 lists 44 on the Ouse between York and Yokefleet, a distance of 43 miles, 33 of them owned by ecclesiastical landowners, most with two or three rooms but one, belonging to St Leonard's, with 29. They were a serious hazard, causing the loss of boats and lives, and a hindrance to trade. The corporation, largely composed of merchants, waged constant war on them, a war not won until the 17th century, by which time the Reformation had reduced the importance of fish-days and there were improved facilities for the transport of sea fish, both overland and by boat from the Humber estuary.

Fig.5 (no.44; foldout, facing) This fascinating map produced in 1891 is valuable as it shows both banks of the Ouse. The section reproduced here depicts four ferries (at Poppleton, Clifton, Bishopthorpe and Naburn), six bridges (Poppleton, Scarborough, Lendal, Ouse, Skeldergate and Selby/Doncaster railway bridge) and Naburn lock.

Freshwater fish was sold at the east end of Ouse Bridge, the sea fish market being on Foss Bridge. All fresh fish had to be landed at the 'fyshelandyng' near Ouse Bridge. In 1567, just after the new bridge was constructed, the lord mayor set up a committee to determine how much land at the east end of the bridge could be spared for the fishmongers and their boats. It decided to lease the land to Andrew Trew and his heirs, who were to make a fishermen's landing place there and pay 16d. a year to the city (*YCR* **6**, 129). In this area, just north of the bridge, fishmongers tied up their boats and unloaded their catch. From here the fish was removed for sale. Non-residents' vessels had to moor further downstream and had to pay 4d. a year to sell their freshwater fish on Ouse Bridge (White 2000, 93). Salted and smoked fish was landed in barrels on the other side of the river at Queen's Staith, though York merchants also imported salt themselves and the dry arch at the east end of Ouse Bridge was known as 'the Salthole' (ibid., 68).

The River Ouse was not important for trade alone. At least up to the 16th century the Ouse and Foss were the main sources of water for the citizens of York, though much of this came from springs in the city (for example, one 'spiede' by the corporation at St Andrew's Priory; *YCR* **5**, 80–1) and was carried by 'burnleders', or water-carriers. In 1552, 1579 and again in 1585, there were attempts to establish a conduit to bring spring water into the city. Nothing came of these plans, but in 1616 the corporation took a quarter share in a scheme to pipe water into the city from Lendal Tower. This came to an end in 1632, but in 1677 it was revived with more success, water being pumped from the river to parts of the city until the establishment of a new waterworks at Acomb Landing in 1846 (see p.14). The water could not have been very sweet or safe to drink. In March 1597/8 brewers and other inhabitants of the west side of the river complained that butchers and tanners washed their skins in the river, and glovers emptied their lime pits into the street which drained into the Ouse above the point where water was drawn (White 2000, 116–17). On the other side of the river, by the end of King's Staith, was the Pudding Holes where intestines and offal were cleaned for the preparation of black puddings. The river was also the place where fish was gutted, and the public privy on Ouse Bridge (see p.54) discharged its contents into the river. The corporation issued a stream of orders in an attempt to prevent the tipping of 'filth and rammel'. The oft-repetition of these orders suggests that they were not entirely successful. Several 19th-century illustrations show men with barrels and buckets near the bank, indicating that they were fetching water from the river (see Figs.9 and 59).

The River Ouse was used by the citizens of York for pleasure as well as for trade and this is reflected in the pictorial evidence. A lithograph produced in 1840 by J.S. Prout and entitled 'From the Manor Shore' shows a family enjoying a picnic on the river bank (Prout 1840, pl.11). A wood engraving by William and Henry Brown (1836), entitled 'The Boat Yard, Manor Shore', shows small pleasure boats, some drawn up on the shore, others being rowed on the water in front of what is now the Museum Gardens (Fig.6). A ship's carpenter called Cornelius Hill is known to have run a small boatyard near the Manor Shore, at the bottom of Marygate, advertising a pleasure boat for sale in the *York Courant* in May 1794 (Taylor 1992). John Varley's watercolour of 1803 shows children swimming under Ouse Bridge (Fig.20, p.32), making use of the bridge's cutwater to keep their clothes dry. Several pictures show anglers on the banks of the river or fishing from small boats (Figs.39, 59 and 61). The corporation held a regular Fishing Day, which may have started as a public display of its authority over the river, but became a social occasion, as the Mayor, Aldermen, Sheriffs and their ladies sailed in decorated ketches to Cawood and back, fishing for salmon. These they consumed, with ale and wine, to the music of the City Waits, a large catch having been ensured by a ban on fishing in the preceding weeks. They returned to be greeted by 'a Multitude of Citizens with lighted Torches and Links, and Huzza's' (Torr 1719, 135). In very severe winters the Ouse froze over and was used for skating — there are several photographs of this taking place in February 1895 (nos.45–6). Bone skates have been found at several sites excavated by YAT, most from Anglo-Scandinavian or early medieval deposits (*AY* 17/12, 1984–9). In the 'little ice age' of the 17th/18th century a severe frost allowed more reckless pleasures: football and archery took place on the river, and in the winter of 1608/9 there was even a horse race on the ice, 'from the tower of St Mary Gate end next the River, along, through, and under the great Bow, or Arch of the Bridge, to the Crane near Skeldergate Postern' (Torr 1719, 91).

Fig.6 *(no.27) This scene is on the river in front of what is now the Museum Gardens. The abbey ruins can be seen amongst the trees at far left and the Minster at top right. There is a pleasure boat, rather like a gondola, and boatmen may be rowing couples who have hired the smaller boats.*

The Waterfronts (Fig.7)

The importance of the Ouse for transport and trade has already been demonstrated, and with it that of the waterfronts. The river was navigable for several miles upstream from York and it is almost certain that it would have been used in pre-Roman times. As it was shallower and wider than today, boats were probably drawn up on the shore. This may also be true for smaller boats in later periods, but the Roman fortress would need considerable supplies for the legion and possibly the water-borne transport of the troops; this would increase with the development of the *colonia* on the west bank, requiring wharves, jetties and warehouses. As trade developed from the late Anglian period to reach its height in the 13th and 14th centuries, these structures were gradually built further out into the river, and the adjacent land was built up with revetments of timber or stone, making the river narrower and deeper; in central York the

river banks today may be as much as 40m away from those of AD 71. Documentary and archaeological research have offered glimpses — often tantalising glimpses — of these developments, but much fuller study is needed. Some further information can be gained from maps, plans and topographical views.

Left (east) bank

Marygate Landing to Lendal

The land between Marygate and St Leonard's Hospital formed the precinct of St Mary's Abbey, and there was a staith at the north-west corner, possibly from an earlier period. The abbey wharf was used by the Abbot, on his journeys by state barge to his outlying properties upstream, and for the unloading of supplies for the abbey. An account of a great flood in 1315 shows that buildings in this low-lying area near

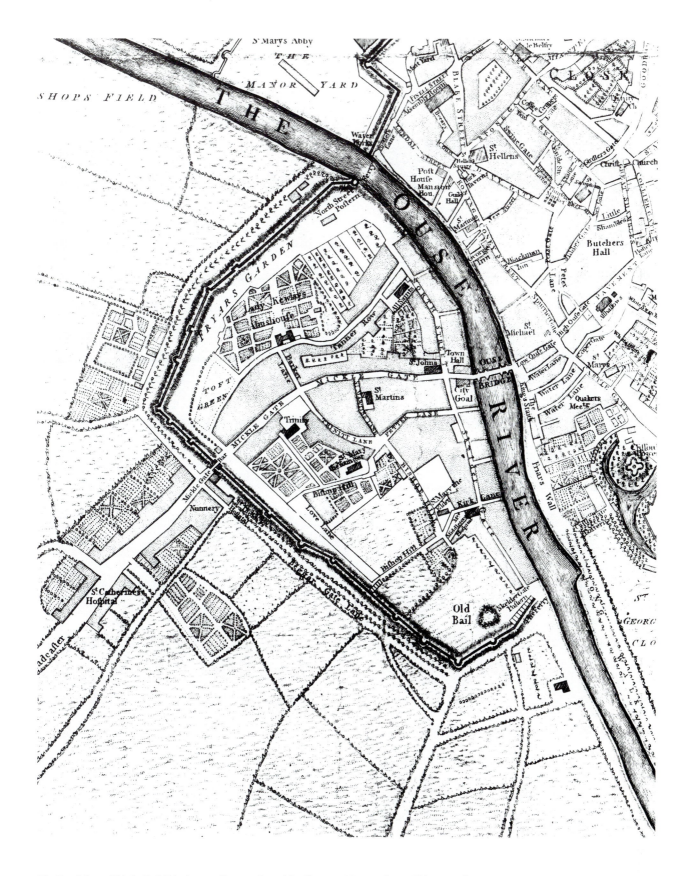

Fig.7 *'Map of York, Published according to Act of Parliament 25 March 1772' by T. Jeffreys. Ouse Bridge is shown viewed from above. St William's Chapel is not drawn or labelled but two buildings shown west of the bridge at the bottom of Micklegate are labelled 'Town Hall' and 'City Goal' (sic). Both ferries are labelled and also the three water lanes. The New Walk is represented by a double row of trees, but is labelled 'Long Walk'.*

11

Fig.8 *(no.36) Nathaniel Whittock's 'Bird's-Eye View of the City of York, 1858' shows the river frontage, boats at King's and Queen's Staiths and the river walls, as well as Scarborough Bridge (left) and Ouse Bridge (right). It is possible to pick out the site of the earlier river crossing near the Guildhall which led to Stonegate and the Minster, site of the* principia *or the Roman fortress (see pp.26–7).*

the river included a brewhouse, bakehouse, stables and a tailor's workshop (Craster and Thornton 1934, 67–8). The staith was the Abbot's property, but was used by others, leading to disputes: in 1377 the Abbey Bursar dug a ditch across the road leading to Bootham and removed the rudder of a boat at the staith, but received a warning from the Mayor that the city had a legal right of access, and had to fill it in again (*YMB* **1**, lviii). Barges continued to use Marygate Landing, and are shown moored there in 19th-century views (no.28). From near the Water Tower (c.1320), but further back from the river, the abbey's mid-14th-century river wall ran almost to Lendal Tower. It is shown on maps by Speed (1610), Archer (c.1684) and Horsley (1694), and appears in Lodge's view of the Manor Shore (Fig.9). By 1736, however, the wall had gone, the foundations being used to rebuild the staith at Lendal Tower (Drake 1736, 577). A boatyard for small pleasure craft is shown in Brown's wood engraving of 1836 (Fig.6, p.10), before the river bank was piled and the esplanade constructed in 1842. St Leonard's Hospital, though standing further back from the river, had a gateway on the side facing the river and employed a ferrywoman. There was

probably a private way to the river between the abbey wall and the city wall at this point; again, barges are shown moored here in 19th-century views.

Lendal Tower and St Leonard's Landing

Lendal Tower was built c.1300 and formed part of the city defences. From here a chain was stretched across the river to Barker Tower on the west bank, principally to prevent vessels slipping away without paying tolls, but also to add extra security from attack by river. In 1631, after several abortive attempts to organise a piped water supply, a scheme was introduced to utilise the tower to pump water from the Ouse. This was not a success, and it became dilapidated. The scheme was revived in 1677, when the tower was let for 500 years at a peppercorn rent, it was heightened to take a lead cistern and water was raised from the river by means of a waterwheel. This was replaced first by a horse-gin and then in 1756 by a Newcomen steam engine. This was rebuilt by John Smeaton in 1781–4 (RCHMY **2**, pl.27 and colour plate facing p.107). In 1846 the waterworks were removed to Acomb Landing and the tower was lowered by 10 feet.

Fig.9 *(no.3) This view by William Lodge shows the steep rise of the river bank on both sides, now obscured by Lendal Bridge. The rowing boat in the centre foreground may be the North Street ferry. North Street Postern can be seen on the left and Lendal Tower on the right. The hospitium of St Mary's Abbey is also on the right, with what may be the abbey's precinct wall in front. The bend in the river is seen from the opposite direction from that shown in Fig.57, p.71. There is some activity on the foreshore and small rowing boats on the river, perhaps being used for fishing.*

Fig.10 *(no.31) The notice in Pumphrey's 1852 photograph proclaims 'The York New Water Works Company Office'. Lendal ferry can be seen in the foreground and the newly built (1845) Scarborough Bridge in the background. The ferry was closed in January 1863.*

St Leonard's Landing (Lendal), as its name implies, was the staith for the Hospital, but was also an important crossing point for the citizens. A ferry operated between here and Barker Tower at North Street Postern until it was replaced by Lendal Bridge in 1862. The landing appears on several views made before the bridge was built (see p.7, Figs.10 and 59, and no.35).

Lendal to Ouse Bridge

The Augustinian Priory, which occupied land between the present street of Lendal and the river, was founded some time before 1278. Adjoining land was acquired in 1344 and 1356, and in 1382 the city granted the friars 'a narrow plot by Aldconyngstrete (Lendal), near their church, extending from a corner of their old wall to their old gate [to] enclose and

build upon, on condition that they repair the pavement there . . . without causing any hindrance to the course of the river'. The Priory was dissolved in 1539 and little remains other than a small section of the river wall (Auden 1906, 171–2). William Hill's boatyard near the Guildhall, shown in 19th-century views, was taken over from John Brown in 1845 and continued until 1971 (no.35 and Fig.8).

The central area of York along the banks of the Ouse was the trading area, the economic heart of the city, and here the banks came to be built up with a continuous line of limestone river walls. Evidence from subsidy rolls and special assessments shows that, with the exception of those drawing their wealth directly or indirectly from the Minster, the wealthiest parishes were those adjacent to the river, and particularly those clustered around Ouse Bridge (Stell and Hawkyard 1996, 2–14; Rees Jones 1987, 260, 265–6; Palliser 1979, 138–9; Wilson 1967, 2–5). Rees Jones (1987, 266) suggests that the 45 tenants of Ouse Bridge in 1440–1, who included barbers, glovers, cutlers, furbishers and mercers, give the impression that it was 'the Bond Street of medieval York where the well-equipped gentleman or merchant could acquire the necessary luxuries of life'. The streets around the bridge contained the homes of the leading merchants, financiers and the trading agents of ecclesiastical landlords. In the early 13th century Jewish money-lenders settled here, though they financed landowners rather than traders. The wealthiest of these, Aaron, lived near St Martin's Church in Coney Street, though foundations and masonry uncovered here cannot be positively identified as those of his house (Dobson 1996, 8; Raine 1955, 150). Between here and the church, land was granted to Fountains Abbey in 1230. At least 40 religious houses owned properties in York, and the Abbot of Fountains acquired several (one at least with resident caretaker and cook), including houses in Skeldergate and North Street. Those on the river front were convenient outlets for the abbey's trade in wool and lead, the rest being leased out for rent. The abbeys of Byland and Fountains had wool-houses on the river bank in

Clifton, on the north and south sides of the present Water End respectively, where wool was prepared and weighed for export to Flanders and Italy (Coppack 1993, 85–7; Kaner 1988, 2–10).

Common lanes ran down from Coney Street to the river bank, ending in watergates which can be seen in several views of the river (e.g. Figs.11 and 57), and are, indeed, still visible today, now mostly blocked. These allowed access beneath the built-up frontage for the loading of small boats (and unloading of rubbish). Raine lists four common lanes leading to the river from Coney Street: Common Hall Lane, the site of the Roman crossing; St Martin's Lane, which ran south of the church and dated from the 12th century; one near the junction with Market Street which ran down to the Swine Landing; and a lane beside St Michael's Church giving access to the Fishlanding. Some, if not all, had locked doors placed at the end after many complaints of 'dung and rammel' being left there when local inhabitants used them to take rubbish to be placed in boats and disposed of downstream. Some lanes are shown on early maps, such as Horsley (1694) and Cossins (1727), and parts of them still exist. There were originally more, but they have gradually been encroached on and built

Fig.11 *(no.26) This engraving by Henry Brown (1836) is a similar view to that by Lodge (no.1), looking downstream. There is a steep bank on the right and mud on both banks, indicating the problems of a tidal river. This picture shows clearly the watergates, the entrances through the 16th-century river wall into the water lanes. All Saints North Street can be seen on the far right.*

over (Raine 1955, 145–58). Excavations and watching briefs undertaken by York Archaeological Trust have revealed the remains of river frontages at 5–7, 13–17 and 25 Coney Street (YAT site codes 1989.1024, 1991.3, 1980.39), and in 1974 the stone-lined passageway from a river-opening of c.1575 beneath 39–41 Coney Street, blocked up c.1700, was excavated (Hall 1996, 76–7).

The King's Staith, immediately south of Ouse Bridge, was the principal staith for the city; it was probably on the site of the earliest landing stage, long before the first documentary reference in the 14th century. In 1377 and again in 1388 the right to collect tolls for the maintenance of the staith was granted to the Mayor, and there are frequent references to work being carried out, with costs given in the Chamberlains' Rolls (Raine 1955, 223, gives interesting details). After the dissolution of the Franciscan Friary, the staith was extended along the former friary shore. It remained the centre for York's trade, though from the mid-16th century most goods for export were trans-shipped at Hull, and early 18th-century artists' impressions of the staith tend to exaggerate the size of the ships there. Near the end of the staith steps led down to the 'Pudding Holes' (see p.9). By 1774 the staith was in decay and, in addition to being repaired, it was repaved and raised higher. Artists such as Farington, Girtin and White show interesting details of activity, but the bustle and sense of importance have gone (Figs.42, 65, 67).

From the 12th century three common lanes, First, Middle and Far Water Lane, originally Kergate, Thursgail and Hertergate, ran from Castlegate to the staith (Figs.7–8). Two remain as King Street and Cumberland Street, though truncated by the creation of Clifford Street in 1879–82; the third was pulled down, only the upper section remaining as Friargate.

King's Staith was enlarged after the dissolution of the Franciscan Friary, which until 1538 extended as far as the castle and had its own landing places. All that remains of the Friary is the river wall, now alongside the Esplanade. It appears most clearly in Mar-low's 1763 view of Ouse Bridge (Fig.37, p.55; see also Fig.7, p.11).

Davy Tower to Fishergate

Between Davy Tower (see Fig.37) and Skeldergate Postern a chain was hung to prevent shipping avoiding tolls, and until the bridge was built in 1881 a ferry operated here (see p.8). Downstream from the tower was St George's Close. While small boats could be beached here, the shore was sandy and shifting, and from here to the confluence of the Foss and the Ouse was open land (see Fig.1), with an approach by path below the wall of the Franciscan Friary. At times this was let out to tenants who collected sand or grazed cattle, but its main use was recreational. In a document of 1587 the tenant had to allow people to walk, shoot or bleach their linen there, 'so that they do not milk his kyne by night, nor tease nor chase his cattle forth of the said close with dogs' (Raine 1955, 199). A century later, Benedict Horsley's map of 1697 shows shirts, sheets and other linen laid on the grass, as does Place's panoramic view from Clifford's Tower in 1705 (no.5). The indent Place shows in the river bank may have been the site of the ducking stool, first mentioned in 1580, when it was to be made 'with all speade', but it may well have been a replacement. In 1607 it was moved to a pond near Castlegate Postern where the water was deeper. No doubt it provided a spectator sport, but the monster still surviving in Leominster Priory Church (Hereford and Worcester) suggests a terrifying ordeal for the victim.

More sedate recreation was provided along the river bank when the 'New Walk' was laid out in 1730–4 'for the public use and entertainment of the city' (see Fig.7). In this way York, like many other 18th-century towns, was emulating the London Mall and the promenades of Tunbridge Wells, Shrewsbury and Epsom by providing an outdoor counterpart of assembly rooms (Girouard 1990, 145–54). Originally this extended from Davy Tower along St George's Field to the confluence of the Foss and Ouse, a distance of 480 yards. The river bank was straightened and piled and the 8ft-wide path was lined with 66 limes and 64 elms (Fig.2). In 1738–9 it was extended by the addition of several hundred yards linked by a wooden drawbridge (the 'Blue Bridge') over the Foss. The path was widened to 28 feet and lined with a further 340 elms. It was described in the *York Courant* in 1754 as 'one of the most agreeable public walks in the Kingdom . . . not unlike or inferior to any of the views in Venice', a view echoed in Nathan Drake's famous Prospect of 1756 (Fig.12), and enforced by a 1742 Council ban on 'persons exposing themselves naked in the water or out of the water within sight of it' (Kightly and Semlyen 1980, 44). In 1782 the Walk was raised and improved using material from the

Fig.12 (no.8) *View upstream towards Ouse Bridge from the New Walk by Nathan Drake, 1756. It shows the steep river bank and sailing barges, including a two-masted square-rigged Humber keel. This is an elegant scene, with well-dressed members of polite society promenading along the Walk, which extended from the city walls to the Foss. It had first been laid out and planted with trees in 1730–4, was extended in 1738–40, and was replanted in 1824. The scene on the left is very rural.*

recently demolished chancel of All Saints, Pavement, and covered with gravel; in 1824 the trees shown in Girtin's view (Fig.58, p.73) were replaced by a more varied assortment of 820 trees purchased from the well-known local firm of Thomas and James Backhouse (no.38). Near the southern end a spring of water, known as the Lady's Well or Pikeing Well, was believed to have medicinal powers, and in 1757 a well house was built to a design by John Carr (YORYM 1999.845; *Interim* **23**/4, 6–16).

Near the confluence of the two rivers, between Fishergate and the shore, were the precincts of the Gilbertine Priory of St Andrew, founded in 1202 and dissolved in 1538. Excavation of the site in 1985–6 revealed the existence of an Anglian manufacturing and trading area, possibly a colony of Frisian merchants, suggesting that there were at least timber wharves along the waterfront (see p.5). In the 19th and 20th centuries the site was occupied intermittently by glassworks, culminating in the National Glass Company 1931–83, which made industrial rather than commercial use of the river, using water and sand from the river bed as part of the glass-making process.

Right (west) bank

North of Barker Tower lay *Bishop's Fields*, an area of open land. Tile pits in the curve of the river at Clifton are mentioned in 1374/5. Views by H. Brown in 1836 (Fig.11) and J. Bell in 1875 (no.39) show that it remained open country with a natural river bank.

North Street, originally continuing up Tanner Row, dates back at least to the 12th century and was largely filled with the houses, offices and warehouses of wealthy merchants. Excavations in Wellington Row and Tanner Row have indicated manufacturing and commercial activity in the area during the Roman period, and it seems likely that there were wharves for shipping along the river bank just below the Roman bridge (see pp.26–7). In 1993 the excavation of a shaft to house a pumping station in North Street revealed a sequence of changes in waterfront management, from a river-retaining wall of the 2nd century through a series of wattle and timber revetments in the Anglian and Anglo-Scandinavian periods to the 15th century. It also showed that the 10th-century riverside was 20m back from the present water's edge (Ottaway 1993, 73–7; Hall 1994, 39; YAT site code 1993.1). Three passageways linked North

Street to the Ouse. One near St John's Church was known in 1375 as the 'lime landing'. It is a pity that the second lane has gone, as it led down to Diveline-staynes (the spellings vary), a staith first mentioned in the early 13th century, probably deriving its name from its connection with Dublin. There were Irish ships in York in the late 11th century (*AY* 1, 190–1), and it is probable that Anglo-Scandinavian merchants traded with their counterparts in Dublin earlier than this. Property belonging to Fountains Abbey abutted on this lane. Broad Lane, the *magna venella* of 1540, was, as its name implies, wide enough for horse and cart, and led from the east end of All Saints' Church to the river. A watching brief here in 1993 revealed a riverside wall, 6m west of the present river bank, with later buildings on the landward side, while another building on the river side of the wall showed that it had been replaced at some time by one nearer the water (YAT site code 1993.8). All three lanes are shown on plans of York between 1694 and 1937 (Raine 1955, 252–3).

Much industrial and commercial property developed along the river bank in the 19th century, and appears in contemporary photographs, notably the buildings occupied by Rowntree's Cocoa Works between 1864 and 1897. The tower block survived until 1988, but the former flour mill was bombed in 1942, the site being given to the city as a waterside garden in 1959.

Excavations in *Skeldergate* have shown that in c.1200 the river bank was only 3m from the line of the present street, but successive revetments and river walls, together with deliberate infill, increased this figure to 28m. A stone wall was built in 1305 after a complaint that the wall of the Franciscans on the opposite shore was causing difficulties for merchants and shipping on the Skeldergate shore. Following this, and particularly in the 15th century, thousands of tons of material, some dredged from the river, were brought in to strengthen the shoreline, and stone buildings, mainly warehouses, were erected. In the 14th century only one lane led to the river but three are shown on the 1694 map after the extension of Topham's Staith. In 1983 a flight of stone steps was discovered giving access to a vaulted passageway which in turn led to a watergate (YAT site code 1983.25; Fig.13).

The Queen's Staith is relatively modern, dating from 1810–20 when the present Ouse Bridge was

Fig.13 Archaeologists from YAT excavating a water-gate at Skeldergate in 1983. In the centre can be seen part of the blocked arch which was the gateway to the river in the medieval period.

built; when coal was brought upstream by barge in the 19th century it was generally known as the Coal Staith. It replaced Topham's Staith, a small 'causey' named after the Lord Mayor who instigated it in 1660 (Torr 1719, 116), which was enlarged in 1678 and became the loading point for butter sent by boat to London in the early 18th century. Prior to this, the shore was for the most part lined with private wharves. Widdrington wrote in c.1660 that Skeldergate (like North Street) had 'ancient built houses . . . which probably belonged to merchants where they might have cranes at their backsides to take up their wares' (Caine 1897, 74). Religious houses such as

Fountains and Selby also maintained a presence here. On the site of the present Bonding Warehouse, built in 1873, stood the Cranegarth reconstructed in 1417 (*YMB* **2**, 81–2), with a timber crane on stone foundations and other buildings including a hall, long chamber and a cellar as well as its own watergate and wharf. Here goods brought by 'foreign' merchants (i.e. non-freemen) had to be landed, weighed and stored until sold, and a fee paid to the Clerk. The goods included linen, steel, iron, wine, spices, dyes and alum, though by the 16th century the principal commodity was lead. 'Foreigners' could only sell to, or buy from, a freeman, and by-passing this regula-

Fig.14 (no.49) Ridsdale Tate's conjectural drawing shows Skeldergate ferry at left (where Skeldergate Bridge is now), Skeldergate Postern and walls at far left as they might have looked c.1700. The 17th-century Dutch-gabled warehouses at Skeldergate, with boats moored outside, were taken down in 1970. There are wharf buildings and equipment for loading boats. The old Ouse Bridge can be seen in the background.

tion by shipping goods directly through the city or landing them at private wharves was a serious contravention of the regulations. As the Merchant Adventurers wrote to the Abbot of Fountains in c.1502, it was 'contrary to Godds lawis and mans, ye being a spiritual man and of religion', and they threatened to take their complaint to the highest (earthly) authority should he not cease and reply to that effect in writing by return (Sellers 1918, 110–11). Abbot Huby's reply would have made good reading, but if there was one it was not recorded.

On a site adjacent to the Bonding Warehouse excavations in 1972 and 1983 uncovered the foundations of a 17th-century sugar refinery whose rear wall was on the line of the 14th-century river wall. A large furnace was excavated, together with rooms containing quantities of the lime used in the refining process. Remains of the distinctive cone-shaped earthenware vessels used in the process were also found (YAT site code 1983.25; *Interim* **8**/4, 43–5, **9**/2, 28–30, **9**/3, 6–9; YAT 1999, 36–7). The site was acquired in 1690 by John Taylor, a wealthy and influential Quaker who, after some years resident in America and the West Indies, had settled in York as a sugar refiner in the 1670s. The raw molasses was shipped to York from the West Indies and refined here until Taylor's death in 1709.

Much of Skeldergate has been rebuilt, especially on the river side, and little remains to indicate its earlier commercial importance. Parts of the river wall are still visible and 19th-century commercial and industrial buildings appear in old photographs but the Dutch-gabled warehouses shown in Whittock's Bird's Eye View (Fig.8) were demolished in 1970. A few paintings also show small sections of the riverbank on this side, and Ridsdale Tate's reconstructions of 15th-century York (Fig.63, p.79) and of the Skeldergate riverside in c.1700 (Fig.14) give a lively impression of the former commercial heart of the city.

Skeldergate Postern to Clementhorpe

Outside the Postern lay the village of Clementhorpe and St Clement's Nunnery. Reference to a man carting earth away from the river bank in Nun Ing in 1575 suggests that there were no revetments, but in 1730 work on river improvements revealed a large foundation of ashlar stone which had probably been the staith for the nunnery (Drake 1736, 249). Place's 1706 view from Clifford's Tower (no.5) shows mainly open shoreline, but includes a boatyard with a boat being built. Later, but possibly on much the same site (Terry Avenue), there was another boatyard until the late 1920s, with a slipway into the river, timber stores, sawpit, blacksmith, and paint and tar shops. This built commercial barges, and may have built the Lord Mayor's state barge, a sumptuous affair, launched in 1733 but sunk in 1741. Beyond this, there was little but natural river bank with a towpath, as shown in several views (e.g. Fig.1), until the opening of Rowntree Park as a memorial to staff of Rowntrees killed in the First World War. Further downstream, the view of the river is now enhanced by the elegant Millennium Bridge, opened for pedestrians and cyclists in April 2001.

Pen and ink sketch of the Guildhall, river wall and watergates by Frank Greenwood, c.1925 (reproduced by courtesy of D.M. Palliser)

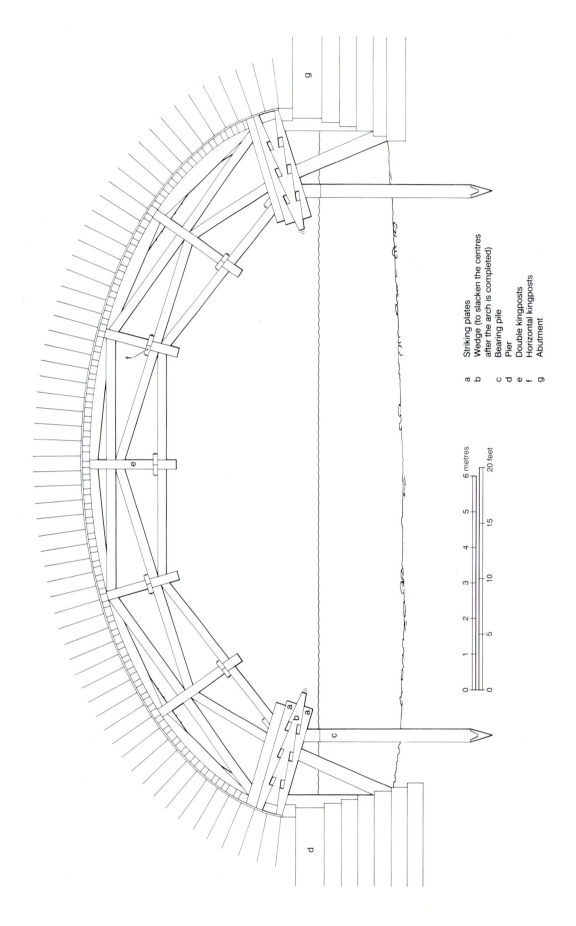

a	Striking plates
b	Wedge (to slacken the centres after the arch is completed)
c	Bearing pile
d	Pier
e	Double kingposts
f	Horizontal kingposts
g	Abutment

Fig.15 *Reworking of a drawing by the architect, Peter Atkinson, entitled 'One Rib of the Centre for the side Arches (63 feet 6 inches span)'. This shows the technique used for building a stone arch. After piers had been constructed to support the arch, wooden centring was built between the piers. In Atkinson's drawing the centring is composed of rafters 10 inches square. The arch was then built stone by stone over the centring, which could be removed once the arch was complete.*

Bridges and their Construction

Bridges have been used for thousands of years to carry people and vehicles quickly and easily over obstacles such as rivers, valleys, roads and, more recently, railways. Bridges over rivers make a slow ferry journey or a long detour unnecessary. The earliest hunter-gatherers would have used natural bridges such as branches or fallen tree trunks to help them cross rivers. When people began to farm and trade, simple permanent bridges would have been built of natural materials like wood and stone. Wooden beam bridges were easy to build but the wood quickly rotted, so beam bridges were soon constructed of stone. Some simple stone beam bridges, known as clapper bridges, have survived to the present day, such as that over the River Dart at Postbridge in Devon which is probably at least 2,000 years old. Such bridges could only be used for short spans, however.

The earliest known permanent river bridge was built almost 3,000 years ago over the Euphrates in the ancient city of Babylon (Overman 1975, 7–13). Its construction is recorded in detail by the Greek historian Herodotus. The Romans, however, were the first serious bridge-builders, constructing a vast network of roads and bridges throughout their empire in Europe, Africa and western Asia. The earliest Roman bridges were made of timber. The Continental evidence for timber bridges is summarised in O'Connor 1993, 132–49; see also Watson et al. 2001, 37–8. The first Roman timber bridge for which there is written evidence is the *Pons Sublicius* (literally 'Bridge of Piles'), built over the River Tiber at Rome in the 6th century BC. When stone was used the Romans could only construct a long bridge by building a row of short arches side by side. Most Roman bridges had several arches, with piers standing in the water below. Roman engineers gradually learnt how to build longer arches and narrower piers which blocked less of the river. They also developed concrete which they used to bind the stones together, though many Roman arches were built without mortar, because accurately shaped stones will hold together under their own weight. Many fine stone arch bridges, either intact or partially ruined, are still to be seen wherever the Romans built roads, though no complete or even largely complete Roman bridge survives in England. There must have been a bridge over the Ouse in York in Roman times, linking the fortress on the north-east bank with the civilian settlement on the south-west bank (see pp.26–7). This Roman bridge would have been 250m upstream of the medieval and modern Ouse Bridge. Arch bridges remained the most frequently constructed type until the 18th century, when iron was first used in bridge-building, making long beam and suspension bridges possible.

Arches are very simple structures that can be built from masonry alone. Arches were used 5,000 years ago by the ancient Egyptians to 'bridge' the gaps between brick or stone columns in buildings. Spaces can be bridged by timber or stone beams, but because a beam is a continuous length it will bend dangerously or crack under a heavy weight. An arch, however, is built up of small blocks of stone. If these are correctly cut and laid, the arch is a great deal stronger than a beam. In fact, the greater the weight above an arch, the more firmly it holds together. The shape of the arch means that a load causes compression but not tension in it. Any weight pushes down and out at the ends of the arch, so heavy abutments (supports at the end of a bridge) are needed to prevent the arch from spreading outwards (see Fig.15).

After the collapse of the Roman Empire bridge-building knowledge seems to have been lost and very few new bridges were constructed, in Europe at least, until the 10th century. Eighth-century Anglo-Saxon charters mention fords rather than bridges, but by the 10th century a substantial number of charters mention bridges. There seems to have been a similar increase in bridge-building in France at the same time. Various possible reasons for this have been suggested, including problems of flooding, the replacement of pack animals by wheeled vehicles and the need to improve defences against Viking raiders (Watson et al. 2001, 60).

Recent research into bridges across English rivers has shown that a surprisingly large number of bridges had been built by the end of the medieval period (Harrison 1992). There are known to have been ten bridges over the Ure and Ouse downstream from Bainbridge by c.1530, thirteen by c.1750–75 when the earliest large-scale county maps were produced and sixteen are shown on the first edition of the Ordnance Survey maps of the first half of the 19th century (ibid., 242, fig.1). In other words, 63% of the early 19th-

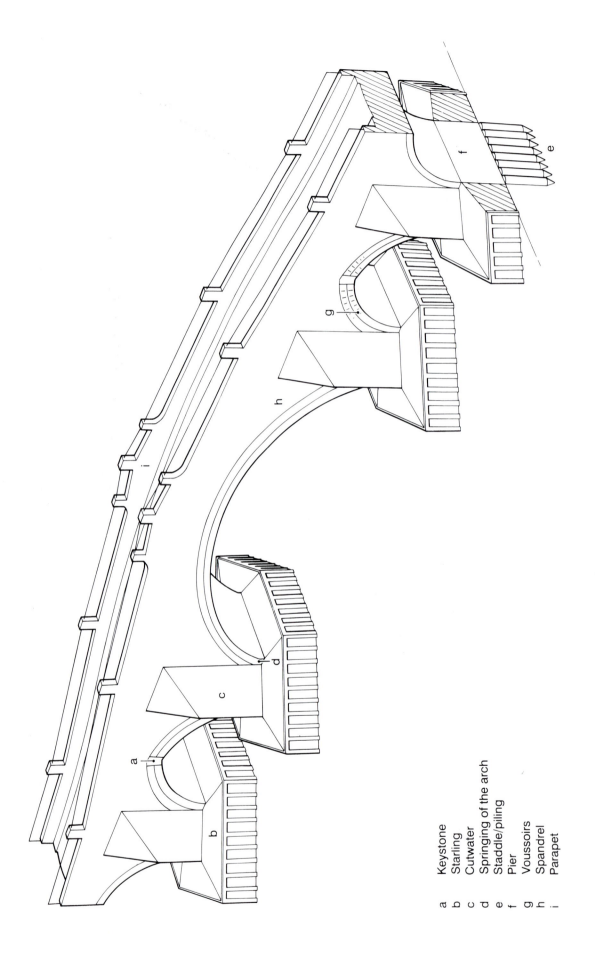

a   Keystone
b   Starling
c   Cutwater
d   Springing of the arch
e   Staddle/piling
f   Pier
g   Voussoirs
h   Spandrel
i   Parapet

Fig.16   *The principal architectural and constructional features of a stone bridge, loosely based on the form of Ouse Bridge.*

century bridges across the Ouse/Ure had been built by c.1530. Medieval bridges were often of high quality. The majority of surviving medieval bridges were originally 9–15ft wide, substantial structures considering that carts as late as the 18th century were only 3ft 6in. wide (ibid., 247). The medieval London Bridge was, according to John Stow writing in c.1600, 30ft wide but the roadway was effectively reduced to c.12ft because there were buildings on both sides of the bridge (Watson et al.2001, 85). Although timber bridges continued to be built into the late 18th century (for example, Selby bridge downstream of York, opened in 1792), from the late medieval period major new bridges were usually built of stone. Of the ten bridges over the Ouse/Ure in c.1530, at least six are known to have been built of stone and only two were certainly built of timber (Harrison 1992, 250, fig.5). Throughout Britain a large proportion of bridges were built of stone by the early 16th century.

Medieval stone bridges, such as the old Ouse Bridge and the surviving Pont Valentré over the River Lot in France, were built with short, semi-circular or pointed arches. Many collapsed because the water flowing through the arches washed away the foundations. An arch only stays up when all the pieces are in place so, as it is being built, the pieces have to be supported. This is done by a temporary wooden arched structure called a centring (see Fig.15). All stone arch bridges were built in the same way. First, the piers were constructed in the river as supports for the new bridge. Then the wooden centring was built between the piers, after which the arches were built stone by stone over the centring. The timber centring had to be very strong; depending on the width of the span, it might have to support a weight of anything up to 2,000 tons until the final insertion of the keystone. Once the stone arches were complete, the centring (or 'falsework') would be removed and finally the road surface would be added on top of the finished bridge. The Romans invented this technique and it is still used today.

The problem of building firm piers in the middle of a river was more difficult to solve. A river bed is often soft and muddy, and the water itself seriously hinders the laying of foundations. The Romans invented a method to deal with these problems, which has been used by civil engineers ever since. They first built a 'coffer dam' around the area of the river bed where a pier was to be constructed. A coffer dam was made of timber piles chained together and driven into the bottom of the river. Two circles of piles were driven in, one inside the other, and clay was dumped between them until a clay wall stood around the site of the pier, to a height above the highest water level (Watson et al. 2001, fig.19). Water would then be bailed out from inside the clay wall. If the exposed and levelled river bed was too soft to support a heavy stone pier the Romans drove piles (staddles) deep into the ground where the foundations were to be laid (see Fig.16). The base of each pier stands in running water so the Romans built streamlined piers with pointed ends which would present less resistance to flowing water than a square-faced or circular pier. The pointed ends of piers (seen on many illustrations of the old Ouse Bridge) are called 'cutwaters' (see Fig.16).

The typical stone bridge in the medieval period had massive piers (their combined width sometimes occupied half of the river channel), big cutwaters facing upstream, and arches of comparatively modest span, usually continuously curved but after the late 12th century sometimes pointed. During the Renaissance many advances were made in architecture. Engineers began to understand the science of bridge-building and learnt to construct longer, lower segmental arches which were much more elegant than the heavy semi-circular and pointed arches of medieval times. The widest medieval arches had a span of c.33ft, but by the 18th century it was possible to build arches c.100ft wide and just 15ft high; these required fewer piers so there was less obstruction to navigation and flood waters had freer passage.

The development of bridges in general and of stone arch bridges in particular can be illustrated by the history of London Bridge. Excavations in London adjoining the east side of the modern bridge abutment between 1970 and 1984 (Watson et al. 2001) suggest a sequence of three bridges over the Thames in Roman times, the first two (AD 50–c.85 and c.85–c.100) probably built of timber, whilst the third (c.100–c.400) may have had masonry abutments and piers, with a timber superstructure. Documentary evidence indicates that this bridge had been replaced by c.1000 and archaeological investigation in 1984 revealed a sequence of Saxo-Norman bridges, the earliest constructed from timber felled c.987–1032. There seem to have been several short-lived timber bridges built between the late 10th century and c.1170, proof of the transient nature of timber structures. It was a churchman, a priest named Peter de Colechurch, who decided in 1176 to build a bridge across the Thames that would last 'forever' (Overman 1975, 40). It was a stone bridge on the site of its Roman predecessor, with 19 short pointed arches and 19 piers, completed in 1209. The bridge was in a dangerous condition by 1800 as a result of the extensive erosion damage caused by water rushing through the gaps between the closely spaced piers. In the 1820s it was decided to rebuild it, and work on the new bridge started alongside the old (as also happened in York; see p.68) in 1824. The new bridge, designed by John Rennie, was opened in 1831; this had only five arches, longer and lower. The new piers took up much less space in the river than those of the old bridge, so the water flowed past them without creating the rapids which had occurred around the piers of Colechurch's bridge. It also made it possible for wider vessels to pass through the arches of the bridge. The present London Bridge, with only three arches, was built in the 1970s.

In medieval times bridges were more than simply the means of crossing a river. They served a wide range of functions including defence (for example, the defensive gateway which still survives on Monnow Bridge, Monmouth), and providing sites for houses, shops and chapels. Their importance in society is attested by the fact that, until the 15th century, bridges were amongst very few buildings to be constructed of stone, the others being cathedrals, monastic establishments and churches. It is known that the medieval London Bridge possessed a barbican or gatehouse, a drawbridge (by 1258), a chapel dedicated to St Thomas the Martyr (by c.1212), houses and shops (c.138 in 1358). In York houses and shops were allowed to encroach on Ouse Bridge, precariously cantilevered over the edge to prevent the roadway being obstructed (see Fig.40, p.59).

The Earliest Bridges over the Ouse

The first permanent crossing of the Ouse was created by the Romans, for whom the river was of vital importance, for the transportation of men, consumer goods and stone from quarries for their extensive building works. Although it is not obvious almost 2,000 years later, in Roman times the Ouse narrowed significantly, just beyond where Tanner Row approaches the river (Hall 1996, 66). This made it the natural choice for the Romans to build their bridgehead. The Roman bridge almost certainly crossed the river from the present Tanner Row to a point under or near the Guildhall, though no identifiable remains of the bridge itself have been found. In 1893 excavations in Tanner Row revealed 'masses of the strongest stonework, which must have formed the head on that side of the water of the great Roman Bridge which crossed the river opposite the Mansion House' (*YPSAR* 1893, 8). Sections of the main Roman road from Tadcaster (*Calcaria*) have been exposed at several points, showing that it entered the *colonia* near Micklegate Bar, then ran north-east to a point opposite the Guildhall, continuing on the east bank of the river to the *porta praetoria* of the fortress (RCHMY **1**, 3b; Ottaway 1993, 39–40). The original crossing may have been by ferry, or, as the river was wider and shallower than now, even by means of a ford, but excavations undertaken by York Archaeological Trust in 1988 at Wellington Row revealed that the roadway had at some time been raised by up to two metres. The east bank of the river was higher than that on the west (see Fig.17), so this causeway must have been made to facilitate the construction of a bridge (Ottaway 1993, 77). The bridge itself may have been constructed entirely of timber, as were the first two Roman bridges over the Thames in London (Watson et al. 2001, 30–2), or it may have consisted of a timber superstructure on stone piers like the Hadrianic bridges over the Tyne at Corbridge and Newcastle-upon-Tyne. It is possible, however, that it was built, or at some time rebuilt, entirely of stone, as was com-

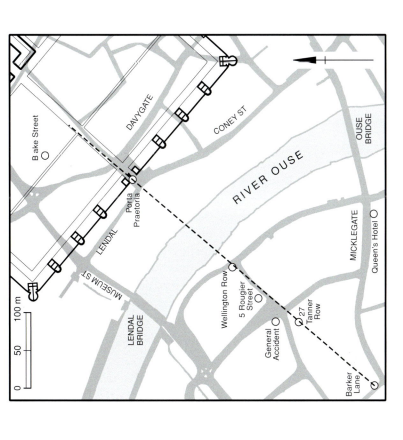

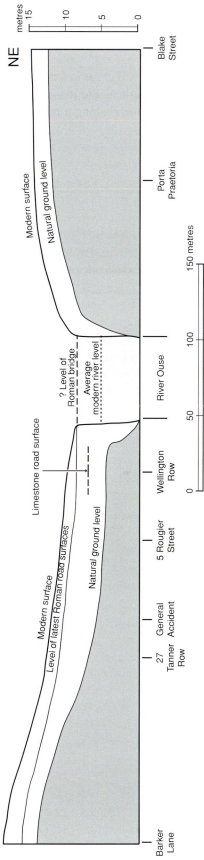

Fig.17 *The site of the Roman bridge over the Ouse. The road which continued the line of the bridge led directly through the porta praetoria and into the fortress and the legionary headquarters.*

mon in continental Europe. Such a structure was well within the capabilities of Roman engineers, and it would be in keeping with the deliberately impressive nature of the defences on the south-west side of the fortress with projecting interval towers (see Fig.17).

It cannot be stated with certainty when the main river crossing was moved c.250m downstream to its present site. The original Roman approach road was narrowed at some time in the 4th century, but Anglian structures and artefacts associated with it suggest, though they do not prove, that it remained of some importance. Firmer evidence comes from excavations undertaken by York Archaeological Trust on the Queen's Hotel site in 1988–9, which revealed that Roman structures underlay modern Micklegate and that Anglian structures followed the Roman alignment. This suggests that the Roman river crossing — and very possibly even the bridge itself — remained in use throughout the Anglian period. In contrast, the remains of 10th-century Anglo-Scandinavian buildings found on the Queen's Hotel site fronted the present street line (*AY* 7/2, 156–7, 200–2; Hall 1994, 34). It may therefore be assumed that the line of modern Micklegate was an Anglo-Scandinavian development and that it was associated with the building of a bridge on the present site. This was probably the result of geographical features: recent mapping of the underlying strata has shown that there was a natural spur which narrowed the river here (Hall 1996, 72). It is believed that the river crossing at this point goes back well into the Viking Age, largely because the area around and beyond the northern end of the bridge was an important part of the city of Jorvik, which had been partly laid out early in the 10th century. This developing Anglo-Scandinavian city south-east of the Roman fortress may have been another factor leading to the construction of the new bridge at this precise point. It may also be assumed that the Anglo-Scandinavian bridge was a timber construction; Viking Age craftsmen would certainly have been capable of building such a bridge (Hall 1994, 34). Remains of a wooden Viking Age bridge have been found in Denmark at Ravning Enge. This bridge was about half a mile in length, crossing a marshy river valley, and was constructed with impressive accuracy. The bridge has been dated by dendrochronology to c. AD 980 (R.A. Hall, pers. comm.; Graham-Campbell 1980, 210). The Viking Age bridge over the Ouse could well have been the structure that lasted until its replacement by a stone bridge in the 12th century.

It is interesting to note that during the debate over the repair or replacement of Ouse Bridge in the early 19th century one of the suggestions was that a new bridge should be built on the site of the Roman bridge. A plan produced in November 1814 by John Watson of the York firm of architects Watson and Pritchett and sent to Benjamin Brooksbank, chief magistrate of the West Riding of Yorkshire, proposed a new road from the corner of Micklegate and Barker Lane, crossing Tanner Row, and then a bridge over the river to join the east bank just north-west of the Guildhall, with a road continuing the line of the bridge to Lendal north-west of St Helen's Square (Leeds District Archives, HE/50).

Ouse Bridge, 1154–1565

In January 1141 William Fitzherbert, Treasurer of the Minster, and described as easy-going, pleasant and popular, was elected as Archbishop of York. The election was, however, opposed by some of the Chapter and by the Cistercian monks of Yorkshire. The latter, with the powerful support of Bernard of Clairvaux, took the case to the Pope, accusing Fitzherbert of using bribery to get King Stephen's support. Though Fitzherbert was consecrated in 1143, the matter remained unresolved until 1147, when a new Pope, Eugenius III, himself a Cistercian, replaced him by Henry Murdac, Abbot of Fountains. The move was not popular in the city, and it was not until 1150 that Murdac was installed. Turmoil continued, including actual rioting and the closure of the city gates against the new Archbishop. In 1153, however, Murdac, Bernard and Eugenius all died. William Fitzherbert travelled to Rome, gained the approval of the new Pope and returned to take up his appointment again in York. On 9 May 1154 the welcoming crowd was so great that the timber structure of Ouse Bridge collapsed under the weight, throwing many into the river. No lives were lost, however, and this miracle was later attributed to the prayers of Fitzherbert. The Archbishop himself died of a fever four weeks later, amid rumours of a poisoned chalice. After reports of further miracles of healing at his tomb he was eventually canonised on 8 June 1227. The Ouse Bridge miracle was a popular subject in York ecclesiastical art. It is shown on an alabaster panel (Fig.18), which formed part of a 15th-century reredos from the church of All Saints, Peasholme Green, found in 1957 and now in the Yorkshire Museum (Willmot 1957). It appears most famously in the St William window in York Minster (no.57; see back cover) and in other Minster windows, now somewhat fragmented, and there is evidence that the same scene was depicted in a window in St Mary's Abbey (French 1999, 1–21, 59; Davidson and O'Connor 1978, 178–8, 181). An interesting 19th-century version, by William Wailes, is in St Wilfrid's Church, Duncombe Place (no.59). According to tradition, the first stone bridge over the Ouse was built to replace the timber bridge in, or shortly after, 1154.

Doubts have been cast on various aspects of the story. York needed a saint to draw pilgrims from the counter-attractions of St John of Beverley and St Wilfrid of Ripon, and a saint needed miracles. A similar story has been told regarding the bridge at Pontefract, and it may be that the Ouse Bridge miracle is merely a topos, that is, a stock story repeated in more than one hagiography. The earliest documentary reference to the event is a 13th-century Life of St William. The writer describes a scene 'dreadful to see and astonishing to relate' (*horrendum visu et stupendum relatu*), as men, women, children and horses floundered in the swift-flowing waters of the Ouse until miraculously saved by the intercession of the Archbishop (Raine 1886, xviii, 275–6, citing Harl. 2, fos.76–88). It was probably written either to reinforce William's claim to canonisation in the 1220s or at the time of the translation of his remains from the nave of York Minster to a shrine behind the high altar in 1283/4. As the former date, at least, was within the limits of collective memory the story could well be founded upon truth. Moreover, some historians have followed Drake in giving the date of the first stone bridge as c.1233–40 but this rests on a misinterpretation: in 1233 Archbishop Walter de Gray was raising money for repairing, not for rebuilding, the bridge (Drake 1736, 280; Raine 1872). It is now generally accepted that the bridge dates from c.1170–80, this being the date assigned on architectural grounds to the oldest part of the bridge chapel (see p.39), which must have been built over a stone foundation. The pointed Gothic arches of the medieval bridge, still visible in views of the 18th and 19th century, are unlikely to have been subjected to major alteration: such arches only began to appear in the late 12th century, but bridge-builders were quick to see their advantages (Cook 1998, 28).

Building a stone bridge could be a lengthy business — London Bridge, begun in 1176, is reputed to have taken 33 years (Watson et al. 2001, 86) — so if the timber bridge collapsed in 1154, it is possible that a ferry or a temporary structure was in use until it was replaced later in the century. In view of the financial problems encountered in 1565 and 1810 (see pp.56–7, 63, 68, 70) it would be interesting to know in more detail how the project was funded. It would be costly in terms of materials, carriage and masons' wages and equipment, and it was not easy to raise funds quickly in an economy still largely agrarian, and at a time when usury was frowned upon. From at least the mid-8th century the building and maintenance of bridges (*brycggeweorc*) was one of the three obligations (*trinoda necessitas*) imposed on those who held land by royal charter, the others being fortress-work (*burhbot*) and military service (*fyrdfaereld*). These were extended in the 10th century, but by the 12th century they had become less specific and their exaction more sporadic (Lapidge et al. 1999, 74, 456–7).

In Rochester, responsibility for the upkeep of the nine-pier bridge was allotted on a pier-by-pier basis to 53 places in Kent; however, the cost of its replacement was largely borne by a single benefactor, Sir Robert Knowles (Yates and Gibson 1994, 43–51). The rebuilding of London Bridge in c.1176–1209 was financed by gifts and endowments, and in the early

Fig.18 *(no.56) This alabaster carving shows the collapse of Ouse Bridge in 1154, with heads bobbing in the river (© Yorkshire Museum).*

Fig.19 (no.51) Detail from Ridsdale Tate's 'York in the Fifteenth Century', showing what he thought Ouse Bridge looked like in the late medieval period.

13th century the fund was being administered by a religious fraternity, the brethren and chaplains of the bridge chapel, until control passed to Bridge Wardens in c.1282–3 (Watson et al. 2001, 73–4). It has been suggested that a similar system operated in York, possibly originally established for the construction of the late 12th-century bridge (Rees Jones 1987, 190–2). Traditionally, the Church also took responsibility for the building and maintenance of bridges, and there is evidence for this in York, certainly in 1233 (see p.29) and again in 1307, when Archbishop William de Greenfield supported the raising of charitable contributions (Raine 1955, 208). Maintenance of roads and bridges was regarded as an act of Christian charity, and the importance that York citizens attached to their bridge is attested by the number of bequests made in wills during the following centuries (Duffy 1992, 367–8; VCHY, 97, 98).

The medieval bridge had six arches, the outermost being normally over dry land, though 'puddle holes' formed there on occasion; only the central arches were used for navigation. Those between, the 'King's Bow' and the 'Queen's Bow', over shallow water, were let for fishing. There are no contemporary illustrations to show the general appearance of the bridge, only a conjectural plan (Fig.78, facing p.102) and small reconstructions (Fig.19). The outer arches may be those shown in later views, with the detail most clearly revealed in John Varley's 1803 watercolour, 'Children swimming under the Ouse Bridge, York' (Fig.20). Here, practical and aesthetic demands are met by the ribbed vaulting and the four orders of arch ring, though some may be later work. Thomas Harrison, who surveyed the bridge in 1810, believed that the ribs were added to give extra support when the central arch was rebuilt in 1566 (WYAS, HE/50). The starlings date from the 17th century, but it is not clear whether the cutwaters are original or a later addition; the picture suggests some alteration. Major changes would have been difficult, as the arch is under the bridge chapel. Views of the east end of the bridge, notably those by an unknown artist of August 1803 (Fig.21) and by Cave of 6 October 1816 (Fig.50,

Fig.20 *(no.84) This arch in Varley's watercolour of 1803 is almost certainly part of the medieval bridge, probably the arch below St William's Chapel. The artist was looking south (downstream), at the arch immediately west of the central arch. This picture shows the cutwater and timber braces with starling below (see Fig.16, p.24), on which children are sitting and standing. The four orders of arch moulding show clearly, as do the ribs beneath the arch, which are possibly medieval, though it has been suggested that they were added to strengthen the arch during the rebuilding of 1566. The starlings were 17th-century additions to the bridge and are not shown on all illustrations; it may be that the water level was high so they were not visible to some artists (see Fig.68, p.87). The tiny barred window just to the right of the arch may be in the former civic gaol or kidcote, which is known to have been very dark. The stonework of the bridge looks rather battered in this view, as it would have been by this date.*

p.66) do suggest some modification to support the buildings over the arch. This arch was known as the 'Salthole', and beside it were the steps leading down from the bridge to the 'salthole grese' on the King's Staith which gave them their later name of the Grecian steps ('gree' or 'grize' is Early English for 'step').

In common with many town bridges throughout the country there were houses and shops on Ouse Bridge by the early 14th century. An Indulgence granted in 1307 states that a collapse of the bridge would endanger property and life, indicating that

there were already houses standing on it. There were 29 as early as 1376/7 (Raine 1955, 208–10; *YMB* **1**, 5–7). By 1435 there were 55 buildings on the bridge, 29 on the north side and 26 on the south. The maintenance of bridges was costly, and houses and shops provided a regular source of revenue. The York House Book records, for example,

Capmaker Thomas Bene came into the council chamber upon Ouse bridge on 12 February 1478 before the mayor and chamberlains, and leased from them a tenement on Ouse bridge . . . Bene and his assignees are to

Fig.21 (no.79) This is a view through the easternmost arch of Ouse Bridge towards King's Staith, sketched by an unknown artist in 1803. It can be seen that work has been done to strengthen the pillar supporting the buildings above, on the south side of the bridge at the east end. There are substantial stone reinforcements to the left of the pillar and also a timber framework support. There are mooring rings under the arch and on the far side, and steps down to the river from the staith which could be used for a small boat, such as the one depicted here. The little cubby hole on the left probably relates to a warehouse which is known to have been sited under the east end of the bridge. The windmill in the distance may be one of those known to have stood in the Clementhorpe area.

have and to hold the tenement for a term of six years, rendering annually to the mayor and commonalty 13s. 4d. in equal portions at Pentecost and Martinmas (Attreed 1991, 139).

Properties on both Ouse and Foss Bridges were always sought after because they were such commercially advantageous sites, with passing trade being funnelled across them. The residents of parishes which lay adjacent to Ouse Bridge were assessed at higher than average tax contributions (see pp.15–16). The Bridgemasters' Accounts list the names of people with tenements or shops on Ouse Bridge as well as their trades (e.g. YCA/C82:11 for 1446/7; *AY* 2/2). As late as 1782 Dr William White noted on his plan of Ouse Bridge the shops of a watch maker, a paper box manufacturer, a trunk maker, a stationer, a fruit and oyster salesman, a cobbler, two cork cutters, an unspecified small shop next to Ouse Bridge Hall (the council chamber and chapel combined by that date) and an inn called the Blue Anchor (Fig.22). An impression of how medieval bridges must have looked is given by the High Bridge at Lincoln which has had shops on it since 1391, though the existing half-timbered buildings date from 1540. John Stow's descrip-

tion of London Bridge in 1598 would equally well apply to Ouse Bridge throughout the medieval period: 'upon both sides be houses built, so that it seemeth rather a continual street than a bridge'.

There is documentary evidence that the bridge needed repair in 1307, the 1370s and again in the late 14th and early 15th centuries. Grants of pontage for upkeep were made in 1403, 1406, 1409 and 1411. In 1502 the bridge was repaved, with a central channel, and in 1526–7 materials were gathered for repair, including ten trees from the Abbot of Fountains. A further £17 6s. 0½d. was spent on repairs in 1556 (VCHY, 515–16).

Although repair work would have been undertaken by hired masons or by the citizens as daylabour, financial responsibility for the maintenance of the bridge fell mainly, and increasingly, on the city authorities. By the charter of 11 February 1392/3 Richard II licensed the Mayor and citizens to purchase lands and tenements in the city and suburbs to the value of £100 per annum to be held in burgage for the maintenance of the Ouse and Foss Bridges, and for the support of chaplains celebrating divine

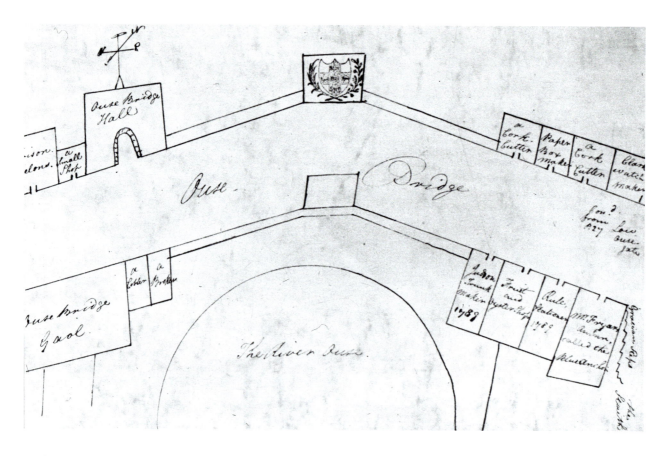

Fig.22 (no.112) *In 1525 there had been several houses and shops at each end of the central arch. These are shown by Place c.1703 (Fig.38) and Toms in 1736 (Fig.40). In 1764 three houses were removed from the south side of the bridge, as can be seen on this plan produced by Dr White in 1782. In 1793 more houses were taken down, leaving the central arch clear (see Figs.39, 42, 50). Dr White's plan is very detailed, giving the occupations of shopkeepers on the bridge.*

service in the bridge chapels (*YMB* **1**, 143; Caine 1897, 116–17; Drake 1736, 205–7; Raine 1955, 67). Income and expenditure relating to these properties were managed by two Bridgemasters until 1626/7, when the office was abolished (*AY* 2/2). The arrangement was similar to that made at Rochester in 1391, when Richard II licensed the purchase of lands to the value of £200 per annum to maintain the new bridge (Yates and Gibson 1994, 50–4); there, too, the income was managed by Bridge Wardens. In York, additional income came from tolls on traffic both over and under the bridge, and by 1280 there was a toll booth on the south side of the bridge at the west end (*YMB* **1**, 123) (see Fig.37, p.55, and Fig.78, facing p.102). The York

House Book records in October 1489 that it had been agreed that any wagon 'commyng to this cite' should pay 'iiij d. to the reparacion of the brigges of Ouse and Fosse' (Attreed 1991, 664–5). The toll booth had a chain which could be used to bar access, possibly of those 'yron bound . . . waynes with great nailes' similar to that shown in the Luttrell Psalter (BM Add. MS 42130, fo.173v) and still in use in 1567 (*YCR* **6**, 128). Together, rents, tolls and donations were managed by the three Chamberlains (later, with bureaucratic inevitability, six, then eight). It was probably true of these, as C.B. Knight said of the Bridgemasters, that they supervised a fund which they 'collected with zeal and disbursed when unavoidable' (Knight 1951, 148).

Bridge Chapels

The Christian tradition of giving help to the traveller is an ancient one. From an early date bridge-building was regarded as an act of piety, and as a result the same masons who worked on cathedrals, abbeys and churches often designed and built bridges. The Pope and his bishops held the title *pontifex*, meaning bridge-builder. An unusual religious order was created in Europe during the 12th century, most active in France where it was called the *Frères du Pont* (Overman 1975, 41). One of the aims of this 'Brotherhood of the Bridge' was the construction of bridges. Its members developed techniques for building bridges which had been lost after the fall of the Roman Empire. One of the most famous bridges built by the *Frères du Pont* is the Pont d'Avignon across the River Rhone, completed in 1188. In addition to London Bridge (see pp.25–6), the English and Scottish Churches were responsible for the construction of a number of bridges, mostly like the old Ouse Bridge with stone arches. Some were built for the welfare of the community, others to make it easier for pilgrims to visit holy places or to ensure good communications between monastic houses and centres of learning. Bridge-building by the medieval Church was not only an act of piety, however. Had it been, 'bridges would have been built in unexpected places. They were not, and it appears that piety and economic rationality worked in tandem' (Harrison 1992, 256). Churchmen were keen to promote trade because a wealthy nation meant a wealthy Church.

The medieval Church was well aware of the religious symbolism of bridges; they were often used as images of the link between heaven and earth. The junction of highways provided a convenient place to hear mass before setting out on a hazardous journey. A 'morrow-mass' would often be sung early in the morning for the benefit of such travellers (*YCR* **4**, 166). In return, offerings made at the chapel would be used for maintenance of the bridge. Bridge-building did not remain in the domain of the Church throughout the medieval period, though as late as the second half of the 15th century a priest in France, Brother Giovanni Giocondo, commissioned by King Louis XII, built Paris's first stone arch bridge, the Pont Notre Dame. It was completed in 1507 (Overman 1975, 49). Recognising the role the 'Church' bridges were playing in encouraging commerce, European traders soon began to sponsor bridge-building for their own purposes and gradually the profession of civil engineer developed.

Every medieval bridge had its cross, but most of these were destroyed in the 16th and 17th centuries. In 1376 documents concerning shops on the Ouse Bridge give their position in relation to the cross in the centre of the bridge (Raine 1955, 210; see Benson's plan of the first stone Ouse Bridge in York, c.1240, Fig.78, facing p.102). It was the patronage of the Church which accounts for the little stone chapels which were sometimes built on bridges, presumably as a means of ensuring divine protection for the bridge and travellers using it. Chapels were usually built over a pier at right-angles to the roadway, jutting out above the river; others, as in York, were erected over an arch at one end of the bridge parallel to the road. A rare example at Droitwich lay across the bridge, with the road separating the priest from the congregation; this must have made life interesting (Morris 1989 368–9; Cook 1998, 40–1). One function of these bridge chapels was to collect funds for the maintenance and repair of the bridge itself. The other function was of a more religious nature, to act as chantry chapels served by chantry priests to say masses for the dead, and for the spiritual refreshment of travellers and pilgrims.

These bridge chapels were not uncommon in England during the medieval period, though the tradition may be much older: altars to Neptune and Oceanus dredged from the River Tyne along with Roman bridge masonry have led to the suggestion that the bridge built at Newcastle by the 6th Legion may have carried a shrine, to protect the bridge or to receive votive offerings. The earliest medieval bridge chapels seem to belong to the 13th century, for example, the chapel on the bridge at Burton-upon-Trent (first recorded in the 1260s). Elvet Bridge at Durham had two chapels, one at each end; one of these survives (see Watson et al. 2001, 110, fig.51). London Bridge possessed a chapel dedicated to St Thomas the Martyr (built c.1212, rebuilt 1384–96; Stow 1603, 23–4; Watson et al. 2001, 109–14). The records of the 14th century suggest that it was during this period that the majority of bridge chapels were built, including those at Nottingham, Rochester, Huntington, Stockport and Bedford. Chapels of the 15th century include those at St Ives and Ludlow (Cook 1998, 40). As all chantries were dissolved in 1547, only a small number of bridge chapels are still standing and even these are much restored: St Ives (Cambridgeshire), Derby, Cromford (Derbyshire), Rochester (strictly speaking, the bridge wardens' chapel beside the bridge), Durham, Rotherham and Wakefield; Bradford-on-Avon (Wiltshire) has a simpler oratory. Most of these were put to a variety of alternative secular purposes after the Reformation. Bradford's oratory, for example, was used as a lock-up and powder magazine.

A brief description of the two surviving Yorkshire bridge chapels may be helpful in giving some idea of the possible appearance and vicissitudes of St William's Chapel on Ouse Bridge. The Wakefield chapel, known as St Mary-on-the-Bridge, occupies a tiny island in the River Calder, its west front aligned with the parapet of the medieval nine-arch bridge. It is an ornate building of c.1350, with Decorated trac-ery on its north, east and south façades, five elaborate arches facing the bridge and the east gable crowned with a statue of the Virgin Mary. At the north-east corner is a tower, originally surmounted by an open crown, with a spiral stair descending to the crypt-like sacristy beneath the chapel. The parapet contained five sculptured panels under triple cinquefoil arches, representing the mysteries of the Rosary — the Annunciation, the Nativity, the Resurrection, the Ascension and the Coronation of the Virgin. It was endowed by Edmund, Duke of York, in 1398, 'to the'entent to pray for the sowle of the founder and all Christen sowles', but had been erected half a century earlier. In the 16th century it was set aside for the use of those afflicted with the plague, so that worshippers at the parish church need not fear infection. The chapel had been badly neglected by the 17th century, the Quarter Sessions Rolls making reference to the 'great ruyne and decay of the stone bridge at Wakefield . . . and the Chappell adjoyneing', and it was later used, among other pur-

Fig.23 *Watercolour of Wakefield bridge and chapel, c.1797–8, by Turner (British Museum, London, 1910-2-12-283, no.241). One can only regret that Turner did not work up his sketches of York's Ouse Bridge and St William's Chapel (see Figs.53 and 66) into similarly magnificent paintings.*

poses, for selling old clothes. The building was heavily restored by Sir George Gilbert Scott in 1847, the entire west façade being transported four miles south to Kettlethorpe Hall and replaced by a replica.

The Rotherham bridge chapel, dedicated to Our Lady, is a much simpler structure built in 1483 in Perpendicular style. It stands on a four-arch bridge which spans the River Don alongside a modern bridge. Probably founded by Archbishop Thomas Rotherham, the chapel is of two bays, again with a crypt beneath, and has battlements and pinnacles. It has had a chequered history. In the late 16th century it became an almshouse, in 1779 the town gaol. In 1826 a new gaol was built and the bridge chapel became a dwelling house, then in 1888 a tobacconist's and newsagent's shop. Finally, in 1924, it was returned to its original use and restored — the window tracery dates from this time.

Both of these Yorkshire bridge chapels appear in old prints as well as being sketched and painted by Turner in 1797 (Rotherham, Tate Gallery TB xxxv, 1; Wakefield, sketch, Tate Gallery TB xxxiv, 10, watercolour reproduced here as Fig.23).

A chapel had been built on the northern side of the west (Micklegate) end of the Ouse Bridge in York in the late 12th century, as shown by the architectural style recorded in detailed drawings by Henry Cave and Joseph Halfpenny and by fragments of masonry (eight voussoirs, parts of a round-headed arch, and a re-used voussoir carved with representations of the Annunciation and the Flight into Egypt) surviving in the Yorkshire Museum (see Figs.31–4; RCHMY 3, 50). It was dedicated in 1228 to St William, formerly Archbishop William Fitzherbert, whose prayers had saved a large number of people who fell into the river when the wooden bridge had collapsed in 1154 (Hutchinson and Palliser 1980, 227). In 1227 he was canonised at the request of the ecclesiastical authorities who wanted a local saint for York. The sculpted panels on the Wakefield bridge chapel relating to events in the life of the Virgin Mary suggest that the York chapel may well have been decorated with scenes from the life of St William, similar to those shown in windows in York Minster (French 1999, 6–11). Illustrations by Cave and Halfpenny certainly confirm that the chapel was richly ornamented (see Figs.28–30, 48 and 73).

Between 1321 and 1331, at the height of the fashion for chantry foundation in York, St William's Chapel came to house four perpetual chantries. In January 1321, for example, a licence was issued by the mayor and commonalty for the appointment of a suitable chaplain to celebrate mass for the soul of Robert of Wistow in St William's Chapel; this chantry survived within the chapel until its dissolution in 1547. The York House Book records in March 1484 that 'John Warde, chaplain, was admitted to the perpetual chantry founded by Richard Toller in the chapel of Saint William on Ouse bridge' (Attreed 1991, 426–7). None of the four bridge chantries was very well endowed, but the mayor and council, with their council chamber also on Ouse Bridge until the mid-18th century, had a team of chaplains directly at their service (Dobson 1992, 321). Having the council chamber in such close proximity meant that the chaplains had to alter the times at which they recited or sang their masses so as not to inconvenience the councillors attending meetings or local citizens crossing the bridge. In other ways the chantry chaplains were dependent on the civic authorities. They received most of their income directly from the Bridgemasters (see p.33) but the civic archives make it clear that when citizens left money for chantries in the bridge chapel, the council often invested a portion at least to buy tenements to produce rents. What was initially established as a religious institution was, therefore, subject to considerable civic control.

In 1547, during the brief reign of Edward VI, chantries and religious guilds were suppressed. The city corporation, already facing economic crisis because of serious inflation in England in the mid-16th century, was anxious not to suffer financially and appropriated the endowments of the seven chantries and three obits maintained by itself. At this time it also stripped the lead from the roof of St William's Chapel and re-roofed it with stone tiles (see p.47). By 1623 the Merchant Adventurers of England were using the chapel as a cloth hall, or bourse; in that year it was recorded that they found it too small 'to walk in' and so they were allowed to use the council chamber as well, the Merchant Adventurers and corporation paying for alterations (VCHY, 482). By the end of the 18th century the medieval Ouse Bridge was a hindrance to river traffic and to commerce largely because of the steep slope of its central arch (see Fig.41, p.59). In 1810 work began on a new bridge and this necessitated the demolition of St William's

Chapel, an event recorded in drawings by Henry Cave (see Figs.28–30 and 48). Little now remains of the chapel apart from the few architectural fragments in the Yorkshire Museum. In 1905 Ridsdale Tate produced a conjectural reconstruction of the chapel and council chamber in his 'York from Briggate 100 Years Ago', which formed the front cover of the catalogue for the exhibition of Old York Views and Worthies

(see Fig.36, p.50). It is, of course, impossible to know how close he came to the reality.

York had a second bridge chapel, on the bridge over the River Foss; this was dedicated to St Anne and housed three chantries. Of this chapel, built by 1424 and in ruins by 1563, there is unfortunately no pictorial evidence (Raine 1955, 68–70).

Fig.24 (no.105) *Varrall's hand-coloured etching of the bridge was published in 1828 but was based on a much earlier sketch by John Carter, presumably the Carter who wrote so vehemently in the* Gentleman's Magazine *in 1806 about the impending destruction of the bridge (see p.65). By the time of its publication the old bridge had been demolished for some years. The picture shows very clearly the corbels on the bridge which were later re-set in a nearby wall (see Fig.44, p.61). It shows a bustling scene with much activity both on the river and on the bridge itself.*

St William's Chapel

St William's Chapel was popularly said to have been built in 1268 as penance for the murder of some retainers of John Comyn, a Scottish lord, in that year, and an oil painting depicting the fight between the Scots and the men of York was found by workmen demolishing the building in 1810 (Hargrove 1818, **2**, 194). There was, however, already a chapel on this site: fragments of masonry now in the Yorkshire Museum have been dated to c.1170–80, and the contemporary account of the events of 1268 refers merely to a fine of 300 marks and provision for two chaplains (Craster and Thornton 1934, 12–13), though there is architectural evidence of some rebuilding or repair in the mid-13th century. The chapel is first mentioned in 1223 (*YMB* **2**, 68), when it was the civic chapel with

an entrance to the adjoining council chamber. At this date there is no reference to a particular dedication. The cult of relics was growing, however, and pilgrims were passing through York on their way to the shrines of Saints Cuthbert at Durham, Wilfrid in Ripon and John at Beverley. There was also much rivalry between York and Canterbury, and the establishment of a splendid shrine for Thomas Becket in 1220 led the York clergy to seek the canonisation of William Fitzherbert, who, it was widely believed, had also been the victim of sacrilegious murder. This was achieved in 1227, and the chapel on the bridge, scene of his most famous miracle, was dedicated to St William, probably in the year 1228.

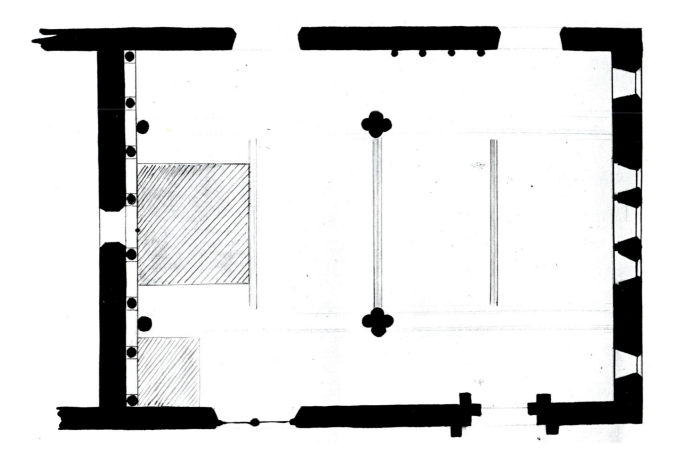

Fig.25 (no.114) *This plan was almost certainly produced, as a historical record, just before the chapel was taken down. It shows the internal organisation of the chapel, which had a central aisle and two narrower side aisles (north and south), each half the width of the central aisle. At the west end was a blind dado arcade, or screen (see Figs.29 and 48). The doorway at the west end led into the council chamber proper; this doorway is shown open in Fig.29. There was more blind arcading on the north wall. Internal dividing screens and column bases are shown in the central aisle. At the east end is a 13th-century three-light window and a small lancet to each side. The main entrance doorway was on the south side. There is a discrepancy between this plan and Abbot's view of 1776 (Fig.35, p.49) over the position of the main doorway. Abbot also shows a small door to the right of the main entrance which does not appear on this plan.*

Fig.26 (no.127) Joseph Halfpenny's etching of the entrance to St William's Chapel, 1807. This archway is of 12th-century date, but the side shafts and capitals are 13th-century. The entrance must have been reconstructed in the 13th century. The triangular spandrels above the arch to each side are probably Elizabethan or Jacobean, perhaps added when the chapel became part of the council chamber and adopted a more civic function. The architectural details are crisp, not a realistic representation of their appearance in 1807 (see Fig.27). Only the side shafts show any sign of wear.

Fig.27 (no.146) In Cave's engraving, published in 1813, the window above the doorway has been removed and the scene is one of dereliction. One door is open, showing an internal screen.

Two flask-shaped pewter ampullae were recovered during excavations at Coppergate (*AY 17/15, 12965–6). 12966*, which is largely complete and was probably made in the 13th century, has an archbishop depicted on the flask itself, his office represented by the mitre on his head, and the crozier and pall which he grips in one hand, the other being raised in benediction (see p.47). It has been suggested that the mitre is of a type which was out of fashion by c.1200 (Wilson 1977, 24, n.25), and that the archbishop may be identified as St William (ibid., 8). The cult status of St William, however, never appears to have equalled that of his hugely successful southern counterpart. Many ampullae and pilgrim badges associated with St Thomas have been recovered (see for example Alexander and Binski 1987, 219–24, *43–65*), including a

large number from the Thames around London Bridge. This suggests that they may have been thrown into the river by pilgrims returning to London from Canterbury, an interpretation reinforced by the discovery of pilgrim badges at a number of major European river crossings (Watson et al. 2001, 110). By comparison, the two ampullae from Coppergate represent the only souvenirs of St William to have survived. Documentary evidence in the form of wills also indicates that, even in Yorkshire, bequests for pilgrimages to Canterbury and to the shrine of Our Lady at Walsingham were far more popular than those to visit St William's shrine in York Minster (Wilson 1977). Ampullae were souvenirs designed for pilgrims to particular shrines in England and Europe. They held holy oil or water that had been in

Fig.28 *(no.148) This engraving by Cave (1813) shows the screen at the west end of the chapel during demolition. The three carved faces can be seen in situ and the fragment at bottom right looks very like part of the moulding from around the main doorway, which had probably already been demolished by this time. Above the heads is the respond of the east-west arch on the north side of the central aisle. The masonry at right may represent the base of a 13th-century lancet which had later been blocked up. Beyond the screen was the council chamber.*

contact with a saint, and were being made in Canterbury by 1171, within a year of St Thomas Becket's murder (Alexander and Binski 1987, 219). It seems very likely that the Coppergate ampullae are two examples of an item being mass-produced in York during the years following St William's canonisation.

St William's Chapel was popular with artists and, as a civic chapel, it is well documented. A plan of c.1810 (Fig.25) shows that it was a simple rectangle, and though no scale is given, comparison with other views suggests an outer measurement (at a rough estimate) of c.43 x 31ft; Dr W.A. Evelyn (1860–1935)

estimated the interior measurements at 36 x 28ft (*York Herald,* 16 March 1909). It had a lead roof and a steeple containing 'a clokk that bells' (see p.48). The chimney shown on 18th-century drawings (see Fig.35) was presumably a later acquisition. The doorway is of particular interest. It was sketched in 1749, again in 1807 by Halfpenny and during demolition in c.1809 by Cave (Figs.26–7). It was a round-headed doorway of three orders, supported by pillars with simple foliate capitals. The arch decoration appears to be of an earlier date than the jambs, and does not fit them, while the break in design at the apex of the outer arch suggests that it has been reworked, presumably

Fig.29 *(no.141) Henry Cave's engraving (1813) gives a closer view of the screen than Fig.48 (p.65), with clearer detail of the 12th-century carving. One arch has been clumsily reconstructed, probably to allow the central doorway into the council chamber to be inserted in the 13th century. This doorway is open, revealing a further doorway in the council chamber beyond. The fine carving on the dado and around the arches is shown very clearly, and workmen are busy with demolition.*

during reconstruction (D. Stocker, pers. comm.). The capitals of the shafts flanking the doorway are of stiff-leaf type, surmounted by rounded abaci, a design unlikely to date from before c.1200, and this part of the doorway was probably constructed between 1200 and 1275. The arch head is, however, earlier in date. The moulding of the outer order forms a 'stepped chevron' similar to the (now reconstructed) doorways of the Chapter House at St Mary's Abbey, which was probably erected under Abbot Clement (1161–84). The central moulding, an interlocking chain, can be compared to that on the Jew's House in Lincoln, and the pellet ornament has similarities with that on a capital in York Minster crypt (Browne 1847, pl.xxvi); both of these date from the third quarter of the 12th

century. The more conventional chevron design on the innermost order resembles that on the blind arcade at the west end of the chapel interior (see Figs.28–9). Two triangular carved panels in the spandrels of the doorway appear to be Elizabethan or Jacobean, added after the former chapel had become a part of the council chamber (Fig.26). The winged cherub's head (omitted by Halfpenny) on the apex of the arch is a motif which became common only in the later 18th century, though its depiction on the 1749 drawing (no.118) indicates that it is a relatively early example (D. Stocker, pers. comm.). The original 12th-century work is of high quality and was probably a late product of the so-called York School of sculptors who, it is argued, were brought together for work on

Fig.30 *(no.139) The interior of the 13th-century east end of the chapel during demolition. Cave's engraving shows the main three-light window and the small blocked lancet on the south side, and three arches of the blind arcade on the north wall. The small lancet on the north side (see Fig.25) is not depicted. The arcade respond with three faces is similar to that on the west wall (see Figs.28 and 48).*

Archbishop Roger's Minster choir, and who subsequently carved several other doorways in the city and county. It appears to have been reassembled in the 13th century from the voussoirs of a doorway of c.1150–75, and provided with new jambs. This assumes, of course, that the doorway was an integral part of the original chapel. At a lecture by Dr Evelyn in 1909 Canon John Solloway, Rector of Holy Trinity Priory, Micklegate, suggested that it might have come from the Priory after the Dissolution; the observation was greeted with laughter, as Canon Solloway was renowned for claiming any odd bit of carved masonry for his church (*York Herald*, 16 March 1909).

The chapel was lit by three graduated lancet windows of 13th-century type in the east wall, flanked by single lancets (see Fig.72, p.94), and by small square-headed windows on the north wall (see Fig.68, p.87). The windows over and beside the south door (see Fig.35, p.49) appear to have been 13th- or 14th-century additions. The remains of what appears to be the bottom part of a window sill are visible in Cave's engraving of the screen at a late stage in demolition (see Fig.28). While not easily datable, it may be the base of a 13th-century lancet like those on the east wall (D. Stocker, pers. comm.).

The interior of the chapel was sketched by Halfpenny and Cave before and during its demolition in the early 19th century; like the doorway it shows evidence of having been built in two stages. It had two side aisles, each half the width of the central aisle. At the west end was a blind dado arcade on columns which may have been course-constructed with the wall, though a broken shaft shown by Cave (Fig.29) suggests that they were actually added. The two northernmost columns appear to be late 12th-century, one with tightly curled volutes of acanthus-type leaves being similar to one excavated from the choir of Holy Trinity Priory, Micklegate, in 1899 and to material from the Chapter House of St Mary's Abbey, giving it a date in the 1170s. There were at least five round-headed arches with upright triangular panels above each capital, similar to those in Holy Trinity Priory and Archbishop Roger's Minster choir. Sixteen stones from here, forming two and a half arches, are in the Yorkshire Museum (Fig.33). The centre was broken through in the 13th century, when a dado arch was removed and replaced by a doorcase decorated with continuous mouldings. One end rests on a large rounded label stop and beneath this the original 12th-

century shaft and capital have been replaced by a small moulded bell-type capital and with more slender shafts (Fig.29).

On the north wall was a blind arcade, shown in views by Cave. His drawing looking west shows three bays (Fig.48, p.65), his drawing looking east shows five (no.138), and there may have been seven or eight altogether; the arcade did not extend the full length of the aisle. It had pointed arches with simple chamfered moulding and stood on shafts which had simple bell-type capitals. The chapel's main arcades, also with pointed arches, stood on pillars of clustered shafts with moulded bases and capitals. A fragment depicted lying on the ground in Fig.29 may be one of these capitals; if so, it shows that they too were of an early or mid-13th-century bell type. The arcade responds appear in several views, and, while those at the east end are not very clear (Fig.30), they are similar to that on the west wall (Fig.48). Here an elaborate corbel on a foliate capital supports three finely

Fig.31 *(no.160) This voussoir is carved with a depiction of the Flight into Egypt at the bottom and the Annunciation above. The carving is very clear. It is probably a reworked voussoir which may have been part of a 12th-century arch in St William's Chapel re-used in the 13th century. © Crown copyright, NMR.*

Fig.32 (no.159) *These two cable-mould voussoirs from the main doorway into the chapel can be recognised from engravings of the arch round the doorway (Figs.26–7, p.40).There is a central moulding and an interlocking pelleted chain with leaf decoration. The carving is remarkably crisp.* © *Yorkshire Museum.*

Fig.33 (no.157) *Sixteen stones (voussoirs and springers) have been reassembled to form two and a half arches from the screen at the west end of St William's Chapel (see Fig.29, p.42). Behind these are stones from a string course, also reassembled. The photograph shows the depth of these stones which cannot be appreciated from the engravings. The bottom part of each of the stones making up the string course would have fitted into the wall. Judging from the pictorial evidence, the two groups of stones do not seem to be from the same architectural feature. Scale 1ft.* © *Yorkshire Museum.*

carved heads, one bearded, and above them is a tri-partite abacus block with a moulding of distinctly 12th-century type (Fig.28).

Views of the chapel therefore seem consistent with the documentary — and even the legendary — evidence, as well as with the comments of Halfpenny (1807, notes on plates xxii and xxiii) and the views of the Royal Commission (RCHMY **3**, 48–50) that the chapel was built in c.1170, with aisles and at least one major sculpted door, but that it was very largely reconstructed with a new arcade and windows in the 13th century. In the reconstruction the west wall of the old chapel and the responds of the main arcade were retained, and the arch of the main doorway was reset on new jambs in the south wall.

A further stone fragment from the chapel, probably 13th-century and now in the Yorkshire Museum, bears a carving in low relief of the Annunciation and the Flight into Egypt (Fig.31). There were altars to the Virgin Mary, St William and St Eligius, and there are documentary references to four chantries including, as might be expected, a chantry of St William (Raine 1894, 70; 1895, 458). The Bridgemasters' Accounts in the 1440s include references to 'carrying the trestle of the shrine of St William' within the

chapel (YCA/C82:11 and C82:13; *AY* 2/2). Offertory boxes to St Eligius and St Barbara helped to defray the costs of chapel and bridge. Records are incomplete, but the extant records for the years 1453–1500 show an average income of 4s. 7d. a year, though offerings varied widely, from nothing in 1453–4 to 10s. 6½d. in 1499–1500 (10s. for St Eligius and 6½d. for St Barbara; see Dobson 1980, *passim*). In 1432 the gold and silver Corpus Christi shrine in Holy Trinity Priory was moved to St William's Chapel, where it was displayed to important visitors on special occasions by the Lord Mayor. There is an inventory of goods belonging to the chantry of the Virgin Mary in 1490 (*YCR* **2**, 62), and a more complete inventory of goods in the chapel in 1509 lists chalices, patens, altar cloths ('som better, som warse'), frontals, Lenten 'baners' to cover the rood and the images of the Virgin and saints, numerous vestments and six surplices for the children of the choir (*YCR* **3**, 28–30). There were four chantry priests, who in 1499 were ordered to dine together in the hall in the chapel and to be 'of good, quiete, peciable and honest conversaccion', and two choirboys, who were provided with food and gowns by the Lord Mayor and Chamberlains (*YCR* **2**, 141, 178). Music was also provided by an organ: the Bridgemasters' Accounts in 1444 list as an expense of the chapel 'for three sheep hides for the organ-

Fig.34 (no.158) The end of the string course from above the screen at the west end of St William's Chapel. © *Yorkshire Museum.*

bellows 16d.' (YCA/C82:13; *AY* 2/2). The chapel had a number of bells. In 1445 the Bridgemasters' Accounts record as an expense within the chapel, 'paid for leather for hanging the clappers in the bells there 4d.' (YCA/C83:1; *AY* 2/2).

For the forthcoming visit of Henry VIII in 1541, Henry Smyth, chantry priest, promised to 'maik a showe of syngyng and other mellody . . . on the leyds of the said chappell' though the king entered the city by Walmgate Bar instead of Micklegate as originally expected, so this may not have taken place. By 1547, however, the chantries had been dissolved. The corporation clearly hoped that St William's would continue as a civic chapel, and Henry Smyth was granted 5 marks per annum to assist the priest, ring the bell, keep the clock and clean the chapel. By 1550, however, the gold and silver shrine of Corpus Christi, valued at £211, had been taken by the Crown, other furnishings were sold and the lead had been stripped from the roof and replaced by stone. The clock, which regulated the city's affairs, survived, and so did its keeper (*YCR* **4**, 166; *YCR* **5**, 39, 148, 167; Palliser 1979, 239). It is not known when the bells were removed, but in 1583 three bells from the chapel went to St Saviour's Church in return for two taken by the city (*YCHB* **28**, fo.102; Raine 1955, 80, gives the weight of these bells). Under Queen Mary the glass windows and altars were replaced and in 1556 a priest was

again appointed to say mass and serve as the Lord Mayor's chaplain. The chapel was again secularised in the reign of Elizabeth, becoming in effect an extension of the council chamber and a repository for the city archives. Sheriffs' courts were held there, and in 1578 the coat of arms of Queen Elizabeth was set over the door. In the early 17th century the Merchant Adventurers used the chapel and also the council chamber as a cloth hall (see p.37), and the Eastland Company held its courts there 1650–96 (VCHY, 482; Sellers 1906; Sellers 1918). Further interior alterations followed over the next 200 years, including subdivision into smaller rooms, and in c.1806 John Carter was complaining of the 'vile use' made of the interior, for 'a Sunday-school, a pillory, fire-engine, lumber of all varieties, filthy cabins, coal-holes, &c.' (*Gentleman's Magazine* **76**, November 1806, 1186).

When the chapel was demolished in 1807–9 some of the sculpted masonry was preserved, and the following fragments are now in the Yorkshire Museum: voussoirs from the south doorway, accession codes HB 430–3, 482 (Fig.32), 504; sixteen stones forming two and a half arches from the arcade of the screen, HB 434 (Fig.33); a moulded string-course, HB 435–8 (Fig.34); a carved stone, probably originally part of a 12th-century arch, re-used, with a 13th-century carving showing the Annunciation and the Flight into Egypt, HB 440 (Fig.31) (RCHMY **3**, 50).

*Pewter ampulla found at Coppergate, thought to represent St William as Archbishop of York (*AY 17/15, 12966*).*

The Clock

Prominent features on illustrations of Ouse Bridge are the steeple and clock on St William's Chapel. The steeple, on the west end of the chapel, consisted of a short square turret with louvred openings and surmounted by a spire (see Figs.41 and 72). The clock has a dial on views from the south (see, for example, Figs.35, 37, 65); the dial on the north side, placed there in 1751 at a cost of £12, first appears in Girtin's view of 1796 (no.70) but is seen more clearly in Halfpenny's view of 1807, at ten minutes past seven (Fig.39). All the views are of the clock first built in 1658. However, there was a clock on the chapel from a much earlier date. A Fishmongers' ordinance, undated but probably from the 1390s, refers to 'the houre of ten [being] smyten of the clok at the chapell on House bryg' (YMB **1**, 223). A proclamation made in 1393 refers to 'the common bell at Ouse Bridge'. In 1428 butchers were allowed to open their shops on Sunday mornings *usque ad octavam pulsacionem campane orilogii communitatis super pontem Use* (YMB **2**, 183). This strongly suggests that St William's Chapel clock was more than simply a bell which told the hours. *Horologia* are mentioned in monastic records between 1280 and 1300, and by the early 14th century these are 'clearly described as complex mechanical devices' (Blair and Ramsay 1991, 128–9). In the 1440s the Bridgemasters' Accounts record as a charge of the chapel, 'for care of the clock for a year 20s.' (YCA/ C82:11, C82:13, C83:1; AY 2/2). There are further references in the Chamberlains' Rolls in the 15th century, and to repairs and maintenance in 1556 and 1576 (YCR **5**, 148; **6**, 138). Most early mechanical clocks had bells but no dials, and while the clock-face in Wells Cathedral, which is claimed to be the oldest surviving in the world, dates from 1392, the earliest specific reference to a dial on the Ouse Bridge clock is in 1593, when the two William Greneups, father and son, were appointed to maintain the clock and dial, and to ring the bell at 4am in summer and 5am in winter, and again at 8pm in the evening (YCHB **31**, fo.17).

The clock was at the centre of the city's economic life, setting the time for meetings and for markets to open, in order to prevent forestallers avoiding both tolls and price regulations by selling or buying before the set time. Other bells, at St Michael Spurriergate and the Minster, performed the same function, but the Ouse Bridge clock served as a visible and audible reminder of the corporation's control.

A new clock was placed on the chapel in 1658, together with a metal plate recording the names of the Lord Mayor, Robert Horner, three Aldermen and the maker, William Edwards, a Welshman from London (YCHB **37**, fo.111v). By now it could be used by York gentlemen to check their new watches, the first watchmaker in the city having appeared in 1615, to be followed by others in the 1640s (YCHB **34**, fos.46v, 60v; Collins 1900, 63, 104ff). It was given a new dial in 1667 (Chamberlains' Accounts **26**, 1666, fo.17; Torr 1719, 121) and was altered to a pendulum clock in 1703 (YCHB **40**, fo.156v). When the chapel was dismantled in 1809 the bell was sold to a brazier, and the clock was sold for 25 guineas to St Michael Spurriergate, later moving to Barrow-on-Humber. The clock mechanism and commemorative plate, but not the dial, are now in the North Lincolnshire Museum, Scunthorpe (RCHMY **3**, 50 and pl.146).

The Council Chamber

The council chamber stood at the west end of Ouse Bridge adjoining St William's Chapel, and was probably built a little later than the chapel, though there is no precise record of the date (see caption to Fig.48, p.65). The north façade of the council chamber appears in many views of the bridge, showing that it had three gables with a square-headed window in each (e.g. Figs.24, 38, 68). It is not visible in general views from the south, being blocked by buildings on the south side of the bridge, so the only clear view is in Abbot's wash drawing of 1776 (Fig.35). This shows two entrance doors and square-headed windows, apart from the large window on the left, which has similarities with those of the chapel. What appears to be an entrance grille to the left of the main door probably led to the prisons beneath. The view suggests, as one would expect, alterations to the original building.

There are no views of the interior, but a good deal of information can be gleaned from documentary sources. The council chamber was on the upper floor with a passage leading to it from the top of the stairs. There were seats for the aldermen and sheriffs, apparently with green cloth and cushions, and a dais at one end of the room for the lord mayor. A reference in 1588 to Thomas Richardson 'crienge with vehement words, and lifting up his hand and knoking the barr' (*YCHB* **30**, fo.19) suggests a wooden barrier of the sort still to be seen in some late medieval Continental town halls, behind which stood the suitors and miscreants called before the lord mayor. The corporation records were originally kept in a leather bag in a cupboard beneath the lord mayor's chair; later the secularised St William's Chapel became the archive repository. The chamber was heated in the

Fig.35 (no.161) 'Old Common Hall' by Edward Abbot (1776). In the civic records the term common hall refers to the Guildhall in Coney Street, and the building shown on the left of this picture should properly be called the council chamber. This view from the south shows the steepness of the road over the bridge, though the artist has exaggerated it. It is the only clear view of the council chamber from the south.

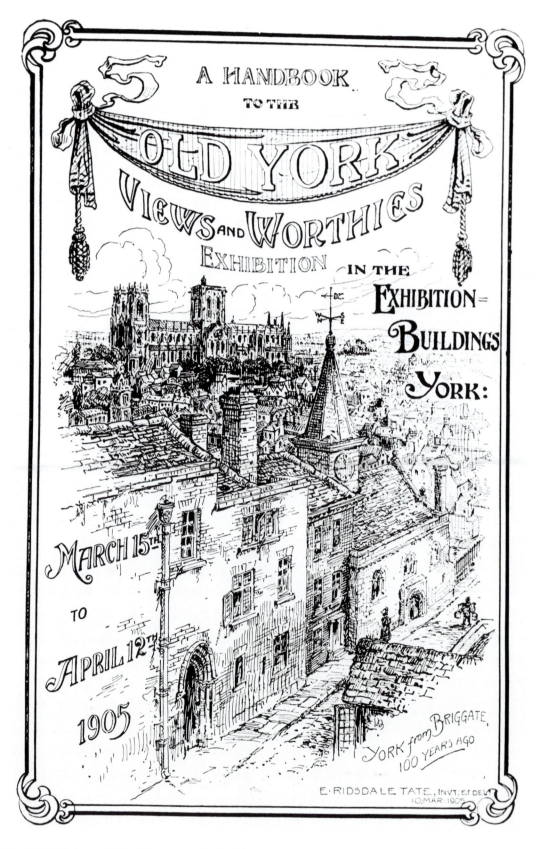

A HANDBOOK TO THE OLD YORK VIEWS AND WORTHIES EXHIBITION IN THE EXHIBITION = BUILDINGS YORK:

MARCH 15TH TO APRIL 12TH 1905

YORK from BRIGGATE, 100 YEARS AGO

E·RIDSDALE TATE., INVT. ET DELT
10·MAR·1905

Fig.36 (no.162) *This is a conjectural reconstruction by Edwin Ridsdale Tate, produced for an exhibition in 1905 but showing the council chamber and chapel as they might have looked in 1805. Tate has changed Abbot's left-hand window into a doorway, similar to the main doorway into the chapel. He makes it clear what a large building the council chamber was and illustrates its stepped roofline, though it does not quite match Abbot's depiction. The building was used as a council chamber until 1807, when council meetings were moved to the Guildhall in Coney Street.*

50

winter, by wood and charcoal until the mid-16th century, later by turf and coal. Meetings were held during daylight, but occasionally dragged on 'until candles were lit'. The lord mayor had a separate chamber, referred to as *camera maioris* in 1375/6 (*YMB* **1**, 32) and probably the same as the later 'studdy'. The town clerk had a room, though some clerks at least also had an office at home (*YCR* **7**, 38–9). There was a separate courtroom for the sheriffs. The two esquires at mace and sword kept the door to the council chamber, while the six officers at mace stood in the passage to keep the petitioners below the stairhead door and relieve them of 4d. each. They wore the city's livery, with new clothes and new colours every four (later three) years. Below stairs the four tipstaves (or 'bluecoats') bore the brunt of the jostling and insults, ready if necessary to conduct evil-doers to gaol. As their name implies, they too wore livery, emblazoned with the city arms; an erring tipstave might be stripped of office literally by having 'his cote pulled over his head'. A connecting door to St William's Chapel can be seen on the plan of 1810 (Fig.25) and in Cave's drawing and etching of the screen in the chapel (Figs.29 and 48).

The council chamber appears to have suffered some damage when the bridge fell in 1565. In April 1566 it was agreed that it should be taken down and the cellaring set up in the chapel. However, Raine says that meetings were still held there. In June it was described as 'newly made', but in the 16th century this was an elastic term, used to mean anything from rebuilding to repainting; it was certainly in use again by June 1566, so alterations cannot have been very drastic. At this time it was painted 'with white and grene panes oyled with the Quenes majesties armes, the princes armes and Citie armes at the higher end'. This suggests that the arms of Mary and Philip were still in place, remaining until at least 1578, when the arms of Elizabeth were set over the main entrance.

The council chamber was the meeting place for what may be termed the upper house of the corporation, that is, the lord mayor, sheriffs, aldermen and the 'twenty-four' (ex-sheriffs, whose numbers in practice varied slightly). Meetings were held in the Guildhall when the 'forty-eight', from 1517 the common council, were summoned to elect mayors, aldermen and sheriffs or to give advice on important matters such as the rebuilding of Ouse Bridge in 1565

(*YCR* **6**, 97–8). The common council could, and often did, make their voices heard. However, the real power lay with the mayor and aldermen, meeting on Ouse Bridge, who took responsibility for the maintenance of order, the promotion of social and economic welfare, and the assessment of rates and taxes. They also attempted to keep a delicate balance between the execution of orders from the central government and the preservation of the rights and interests of the citizens of York, and to maintain the rights of the civic government against perceived threats from other local courts and authorities.

Though civic matters were conducted with much display and ceremony, the council chamber was not a centre for entertainment and hospitality. The lord mayor was expected to live within the city and to entertain visiting dignitaries in his own house and at his own cost, except for the wine. During his mayoralty the civic plate was kept there; at the commencement of his year in office he would enter a bond for £500 and an audit would be taken on his departure (*YCHB* **35**, fos.154v–155). On his elevation to the aldermanic bench in 1635 Henry Thompson added a banqueting hall to his house, and large quantities of silver and napery appear in aldermanic inventories (e.g. James Birkby, 1610, Borthwick Institute CPH 767). Charles I was entertained by William Allanson in 1633, and in 1639 he was provided with a 'sumptuous Banquett' at the Herbert House, Pavement, home of Roger Jaques (*YCHB* **33**, fo.211; **36**, fo.28); Alderman Edward Thompson, however, asked to vacate a house for the future James II in 1679, retaliated by removing all his furniture (Kightly and Semlyen 1980, 22). The problem of suitable accommodation for civic hospitality was finally resolved by the building of the Mansion House in 1725–30.

If the council chamber was not regarded as suitable for entertainment, the bridge and its approaches were used on occasion. Distinguished visitors, royalty in particular, were usually met by the sheriffs at the bounds of the Ainsty — Tadcaster Bridge or Skip Bridge near Green Hammerton — and were then greeted officially by the lord mayor and corporation at Micklegate Bar before progressing through the city centre by way of Ouse Bridge. Normally the bridge itself played no significant part in this, though there were exceptions. In 1486 Henry VII, after receiving the city keys from Ebrauk (legendary founder of York) at the Bar and a rain of rose water at the foot of

Micklegate, was greeted 'on the hight of Ousebrigg' by six kings, representing the six previous Henries. These passed a sceptre to Solomon, who presented it to the king, with much lengthy, flattering and alliterative verse. Across the bridge there were to be more displays, with a hail of comfits and a snowstorm of wafers (*YCR* **1**, 155–9). In 1617 James I was greeted on the bridge by a colourful and possibly alarming figure representing the River Ouse who pleaded the cause for navigational improvement in 25 lines of verse (*YCHB* **34**, fo.120). In both cases the situation was unusual: in 1486 councillors, some of whom were former protegés of Richard III, were uncomfortably aware that they had backed the wrong man at Bos-

worth Field, and were therefore especially keen to make a good impression on Henry Tudor; in 1617 they hoped for the king's support in schemes to improve river communications (see p.5). Otherwise the bridge was merely a stage in the royal progress through the city, though a massive triumphal arch, 64ft high, was erected there, together with others on Lendal Bridge and in St Leonard's Place, for the visit of the future Edward VII in 1866 (Evelyn Collection 1213; illustrated in Kightly and Semlyen 1980, 56). Nevertheless, Ouse Bridge, with its chapel, council chamber, civic prison and even its clock and weathervane, provided a focal point for government, trade and communications within the city.

The Prisons

Situated unhappily beneath the council chamber were the two civic prisons, the mayor's and the sheriffs' kidcotes. The earliest known reference is to 'le Kydcote' in a will of 1396 (Borthwick Institute, Register of Wills **1**, fo.102r), though the prisons may have existed even earlier. Their position is indicated by a few small windows shown in views of the north side of the bridge (see Figs.20 and 72). Each prison had two divisions — for men and women — and they were on two levels, the sheriffs' being the lower one, though in practice this was often reserved for the more recalcitrant prisoners. A door shown in Abbot's view of the council chamber (Fig.35) but not on the plan of c.1810 (Fig.25) may have led to this lower floor. There are no views of the interior. There is, however, documentary evidence in the civic records and lodged indelibly in the memories of the inmates. Needless to say, conditions were appalling: filthy,

dark, verminous, cold and damp, and on the lower floor even dangerous. In January 1732 the river rose some nine feet overnight 'and had liked to have drowned the poor prisoners in the low goal [sic]' (Drake 1736, 281). In c.1594 three women 'took their death with cold' after a winter night in the gaol without bedding (Morris 1872–7, 302). The prison had stout doors with locks whose keys alone were sufficiently weighty to inflict injury (*YCR* **2**, 77). In 1578 six pairs of bolts, two pairs of manacles and two iron collars were made 'for due correccon of persons in the Sheriffs Kidcotes' (*YCR* **7**, 184), and the gaol housed a set of stocks. The doors were repaired and strengthened in 1588/9, 1596 and 1598.

The alterations to the kidcote and the chapel 'for the more straite keepinge of the presoners their' (*YCHB* **29**, fo.16) came at a time when the corporation, in somewhat reluctant compliance with orders from the High Commission and the Council in the North, was attempting to suppress Catholic recusancy in the city. Elizabethan anti-Catholic laws not only increased the pressure of numbers in the prisons, but faced the authorities with a more difficult type of prisoner. In 1579 prisoners in the upper rooms level with the roadway had been allowed to 'angle' with baskets for food and money from passers-by (*YCR* **8**, 22–3), but in 1583/4 the sheriffs found the prisoners to be in possession of mass books, pictures, holy water, beads, wax candles and unlawful books, and a horrified city council put a stop to the practice (*YCHB* **28**, fo.129); it was later resumed and continued into the 18th century. In 1598 William Hutton, a prisoner in the kidcote, claimed that there were 25 recusants there, fourteen men and eleven women; that of 30 women there over the last fourteen years fourteen had died; and that some recusants were kept there for up to ten or twelve years, while one Thomas Bell was kept in the stocks for the whole of a winter of frost and snow. In 1572 women accused of stealing the heads of executed rebels from stakes above the prison were placed in the lower gaol 'where they could not see at noon time of the day to eat their meat without a candle, their beds being loathsome with filth by reason of drouge and very evil noyed with thieves and naughty packs' until the alleged theft was proved to have been impossible (Morris 1872–7, 302).

A century later, in 1661–2, members of the Society of Friends were also imprisoned in the kidcote, some of them for two or three months, for refusal to take oaths; they too complained of extreme discomfort, though conditions were worse in the Castle, where five died. In 1682 John Taylor, the Quaker sugar refiner (see p.21), was imprisoned for non-payment of fines, but his neighbours secured his release on the grounds that the prosecution was malicious. The informer withdrew his evidence but the advocate was later sent to the kidcote instead. The case is an interesting reflection of the scandals in London and other towns, where dissenters were suffering from the unscrupulous abuse of the judicial system by highly organised common informers (Besse 1753, 103–6; Sessions and Sessions 1971, 6; Scott 1991, 24).

Hutton's notes provide the most revealing picture of conditions in the kidcote, though some allowance must be made for exaggeration in a work produced as a contribution to Catholic martyrology at a time of heightened religious tension. As the civic prison, the kidcote normally housed offenders against local regulations. Men charged with more serious offences might be sent there pending further enquiries or a decision on which court should try them. William Hyndley, master mason of the Minster and responsible for the organ screen, was committed in 1491 pending enquiry into his part in the murder of John Partrik, a tiler, during a particularly turbulent period in the city's history. In later years, however, the principal offences were disorderly behaviour, failure to pay local rates or obey injunctions, or abuse of office. Assault on civic officials was common. Occasionally this took physical form; more often it was verbal, and the language imaginative. The length of sentence is rarely given; the offender would be sent down until he apologised or made amends, and a few nights in the kidcote usually had the required effect. To the discomfort was added the cost; a scale of charges laid down in 1673 shows prisoners paying for board and lodging, making payments to the gaoler and the turnkey, and facing a fine of 12d for 'any unlawfull swearing, raling, reasoning, or undecent conference of any matters whatsoever' (Drake 1736, 195). This fine went towards the support of the poor prisoners in the lower gaol, while frequent charitable gifts and bequests by wealthy citizens went some way towards mitigating the severity of conditions for the poorer prisoners literally beneath the feet of members of the corporation.

Opposite the council chamber another gaol, principally for debtors, stood over an extension of the bridge arch, which was built specifically to support it. According to Drake both gaol and arch were erected in 1575, but the date given by Torr for this structure is 1655, the earlier gaol having been built 'anenst the Kidcoate' in 1574. The city records also refer to a 'new house' being used for prisoners in 1574, though its precise position is not clear (Drake 1736, 181; Torr 1719, 81, 112; *YCR* **7**, 98). In 1724 the debtors' gaol was rebuilt, paid for jointly by the City and the Ainsty, and 'considering the straitness of the place it stands on, is as commodious and convenient as most goals [sic] in England' (Drake 1736, 181). This building and the arch beneath it can be seen in 18th-century views of the bridge from the south (e.g. Fig.37). This in turn was taken down after 1802, when a new prison was built near the Old Baile by Peter Atkinson.

The *Maison Dieu*

A small *maison dieu*, or almshouse, stood at the west end of Ouse Bridge opposite St William's Chapel. Medieval York probably had 22 hospitals and alms-houses at any one time (a figure second only to London, with 25), though the approximate sites of 31 have been recorded (Palliser 1979, 222; Brunskill 1960, 7; *AY* 11/1, 18–19, fig.11). Raine says that it was for the sick and infirm of both sexes, but documents of 1490, 1590 and 1596 refer to women only. The date of foundation is unknown, but apparently in the 13th century it was mismanaged and fell into disuse before being re-founded in 1302 (Raine 1955, 213). It is mentioned in several 14th- and 15th-century wills, and as the city *maison dieu* it received 10s. 0d. a year from the city chamber. The main income was from the farm and rents from some seventeen properties within the city; in c.1377 this amounted to £4 12s. 2d., which was to be distributed to the inhabitants in bread each Friday for ever (*YMB* **1**, 25–6). In the 1440s the Bridgemasters' Accounts record 'And to poor women in the *maison dieu* on Use Bridge 7s.' (YCA/C82:10, C82:13; *AY* 2/2). In 1490 a rent of 2s. 6d. had remained unpaid for eighteen years; it was settled on payment of 20s. 0d. and a future annual sum of 12d. (Knight 1944, 362). Otherwise there is little information, and none relating to the inmates or their living conditions. Though fourteen hospitals were closed during the 16th century, the Ouse Bridge *maison dieu* was still in use in 1590 and still standing, though probably in some disrepair, in 1596 (Palliser 1979, 222; *YCHB* **30**, fo.206; **31**, fo.251). It is not certain when it was finally closed. The last reference to it is 25 February 1596/7 (*YCHB* **31**, fo.251), when it was to be 'viewed'.

In 1367 'Novae latrinae, Anglice, les New Pryves' were installed in an arch of the bridge below the *maison dieu*. This was not an unusual installation: London Bridge had a public privy by 1306 which, according to Stow, fell into the Thames in 1481, drowning five men (Watson et al. 2001, 99). In the 1440s the Bridgemasters' Accounts record 'And for the wardens of the house of the latrines and the light of the same on Use Bridge for a year 6s. 8d.' (YCA/C82:10, C82:11, C82:13, C83:1; *AY* 2/2). By 1544 the Ouse Bridge privies had an attendant, Alice Grethede, who was paid 2s. per year 'for kepying cleyn the pyssing holles' and ensuring that no one should 'caste no fylthe nor other ramell furthe of the same into the watter of Owse' (Raine 1955, 213; *YCR* **4**, 122). In 1578 Robert Stephenson was allowed 8s. off his rent of 10s. for a house on Ouse Bridge for cleaning the common privies (White 2000). In March 1579/80 it was decided that all privies on the Ouse should be removed (*YCHB* 27, fo.228v).

Ouse Bridge, 1565–1810

By January 1563/4 there was much concern for the safety of Ouse Bridge, and the corporation was planning to take on masons and to bring stone from the ruins of Holy Trinity, Micklegate, and Foss Bridge Chapel for repairs. Costs proved high, however, and York was poor; in April 1564 the faults in the bridge were viewed again, to see if 'it will hold and contynew still as it is without great jeoperdy' (*YCR* **6**, 73, 82). The answer came on 6 January 1564/5, when, after a frost and a sudden thaw, ice floes carried on the swollen waters of the Ouse caused the central pier and arches of the bridge to collapse, bringing down twelve houses and resulting in twelve deaths (Torr 1719, 78; Palliser 1979, 3). The city was thus split in two, and the only bridge over the Ouse between Boroughbridge and the sea had been lost. A ferry service was organised, with two large boats and a small one, at a return fare of 1d. for man and horse, ½d. for a foot passenger, York citizens being transported free of charge. This was soon replaced by a pontoon bridge, boats being hired and later bought for the purpose, at a total cost for the year of £179 13s. 9½d.

Fig.37 (no.65) *A splendid view of the bridge from the south by William Marlow, c.1763. It shows very clearly the buildings associated with the bridge, from left to right (west to east): the toll booth (the small stone building, gable end on, next to the tree); the brick-built debtors' prison, rebuilt in 1724 and taken down after 1802; the council chamber and St William's Chapel on the north side of the bridge are almost hidden by the prison; on the right is a single building still encroaching on the central arch (cf. Fig.38). The other buildings on the right are private rather than public. The picture shows clearly the river walls on both sides. The wall with massive buttresses on the right is the river wall of the Franciscan Friary, built c.1290. In the foreground at right is the Davy Tower, from which a chain could be stretched across the river to the Crane Tower to prevent boats coming up the river without paying the toll (Raine 1955, 21, 28). In time of crisis the chain also served as a continuation of the city defences.*

Meanwhile, the corporation considered how to raise money for rebuilding the stone bridge. The possibility of leasing corporation property was discussed, but eventually the common council agreed that a rate of £400 should be levied on York citizens. In the event, only £174 was raised, and individual donations were needed, such as that of £100 by Jane Hall, widow of Alderman Robert Hall, duly recorded on a brass plate affixed to the north side of the new bridge in 1566 and revealing an interesting continuance of medieval Catholic tradition in Protestant England:

By works Lady Jane Hall
Her Faith doth shewe
Giveing one hundred pounds
This Bridg to renewe
(Keep c.1680, 163, quoted in Palliser 1979, 245).

As Professor Palliser points out, this version is different from that given in Drake (1736, 280). Technical advice was also needed, and in June the corporation wrote to Ralph Hall, one of the city's MPs, and to Sir Martin Bowes, a York man who was now a successful goldsmith and alderman in London and already known as a benefactor to his native city, asking for assistance. Sir Martin replied that the Corporation of London would send Thomas Harper, who had worked on London Bridge, York paying his expenses only, but adding 'I pray you make moche of hym for

he is an honest man'. Unfortunately he could only be spared for one month, 'and moche a doo I had to gett that space for hym to helpe you' (letter from Sir Martin Bowes, 7 July 1565; *YCR* **6**, 102). The exact nature of Harper's advice is not recorded, but on his return to London in August, the Lord Mayor of York, John Bean, expressed full satisfaction and gave him £5. In the meantime work continued on the construction of a caisson to hold back the water so that masons could construct foundations for the piers. However, the rise and fall of the water was creating difficulties, and on 1 September the labourers were discharged and work on the bridge was suspended until the following spring. Building was normally a seasonal activity, undertaken only between Easter and Michaelmas or, in practice, between Candlemas (2 February) and All Saints' Day (1 November), and in the event the winter of 1565–6 proved to be particularly severe throughout western Europe.

At a meeting of the full council on 10 April 1566 it was agreed that the new bridge should be built with one large central arch, 'accordyng as by consell of the most expert and politick men it is thought most expedient, ready, suerest and cheapest' (*YCR* **6**, 112–13). John Todd, carpenter, undertook the construction of the 'centrell', or timber frame for the stone arch (see Fig.15), and Christopher Walmesley was appointed as master mason. Stone was collected from

Fig.38 *(no.63) This view downstream, from the north, by Francis Place is the earliest known drawing of the old Ouse Bridge (1703). It shows buildings on the central arch of the bridge which were removed by the end of the 18th century, some in the 1760s and more in 1793, and therefore do not appear on most pictures. These structures were built out over the river to prevent them taking up too much of the road on the bridge. Looking through the central arch, the view just the other side of the bridge is surprisingly rural. This picture shows the cutwaters and starlings (see Fig.16) very clearly and the shape of the central arch is probably accurately portrayed.*

St George's Chapel, St Anne's Chapel on Foss Bridge, Holy Trinity Priory and the ruinous 'Bichedoughter' tower near the Old Baile, and a request was made to the Archbishop for masonry from either St Mary's Abbey or from his own former palace. Newly worked facing stone was supplied by William Oldred from quarries at Tadcaster. Raine comments that when the bridge was taken down in 1810 a number of inscribed stones and old tombstones were found in the remains of the arch (Raine 1955, 221). By the end of October, iron railings were being ordered for the bridge, and on 7 November the pontoon bridge was dismantled, some of the timber being used for the repair or rebuilding of the seventeen small shops and houses which were available for rent by 8 January 1566/7 (*YCR* **6**, 120, 121–2). 'Pyles', or projecting jetties (in modern terms, starlings; see Fig.16), were added to the north side of the piers 'for saveguard of the pyllars frome raige of the watters . . . in like form as it is at London' (*YCR* **6**, 119; cf. Watson et al. 2001, 88–9). These took the force of the river and protected the piers from collisions with boats or debris, and they needed constant checks. They were repaired in 1594 and again in 1632, when planks were nailed against them, the spaces being filled with stones (*YCHB* **35**, 171v and 177v). They can be seen in several views of the bridge from upstream, notably those by Place (1703), Toms (1736) and Varley (1803) (Figs.20, 38, 40). Debris from the fallen bridge remained a hindrance and possible hazard to shipping: in June 1567 the corporation ordered that it should be cleared by common day work; in June 1568 any freeman willing to raise stones might keep them for his own use; in August of that year more common day works were ordered, requiring 'xl laborars a day at the least' (*YCR* **6**, 128, 137, 139). As late as 1581 the preamble to the Merchant Adventurers' charter still refers to the problem (Sellers 1918, 244), though there may have been some special pleading here.

The necessity for repair, strengthening and river-clearance, along with a misreading of the date of the collapse of the old bridge ('January 1564' for 'January 1564/5') has led some writers to assume that rebuilding was an unduly lengthy process (Hargrove 1818, **2**, pt.1, 192; Davies 1880, 200; Knight 1944, 409–10). It is clear from the city records, however, that the bridge was finished and usable by November 1566, 22 months after the original disaster, the actual rebuilding being done in six months. Considering the problems of fundraising in a city only just recovering from a lengthy economic recession (Palliser 1979, *passim*), of finding skilled workmen and suitable materials, and of avoiding the obvious dangers of working in the river during the winter months, the work was completed with commendable speed. The building of the new Ouse Bridge in 1810–20 and of Layerthorpe Bridge in the 1990s both took longer.

The decision to replace the original central arches by a single stone bow was a sensible one, in that it obviated the need to build a central pier in relatively deep water and facilitated the passage of river traffic, though the masts of sailing boats still had to be lowered, as shown in illustrations (see, for example, Figs.39 and 68). It was also, for its time, a fairly bold design. Measurements given for the arch vary, but Joseph Halfpenny, who measured it in c.1807, states: 'Taking it from the spring of the arch, it measures eighty-one feet in width, and to the key-stone twenty-six feet and three inches in height: the soffit is sixteen feet and nine inches in breadth' (Halfpenny 1807, note to pl.XXI). It was much admired for its 'catenarian' design, that is, the arc (inverted) formed by a chain suspended from two points of equal height. Robert Davies (town clerk 1828–48) believed, however, that this had come about by accident, citing his friend Charles Wellbeloved, who said that when the arch was taken down in the early 19th century, he had been taken in a boat by Abraham Craven, the builder of the new bridge,

to inspect closely the structure of the abutments, and they saw plainly that there had been a gradual displacement of a portion of the masonry, near the springing of the arch on both sides, sufficient to account satisfactorily for the peculiar curve of the arch, which they could have no doubt had been originally designed to be segmental. By this displacement, which might have been occasioned by the premature removal of the centre framework, or by some fault of the mortar or workmanship, the arch had gradually, and probably with imperceptible slowness assumed the 'catenarian' form, which caused it to be the object of so much admiration' (Davies 1880, 200).

Halfpenny had already made a similar comment; on measuring the arch, he found that 'a segment of a circle will pass through each point, except nearly halfway between the spring and the crown of the arch; a pressure having forced the arch a little out of its curve' (Halfpenny 1807, note on pl.XXI). The mathematical formula for a catenary was not published until 1691,

Fig.39 (no.90) This 1807 etching by Halfpenny shows the north elevation of the bridge and the chapel from upstream. This is a valuable picture as it shows clearly the alterations which had been made to the arch east of the central one (a rounded and a pointed arch can be seen together at left). No two arches of the bridge are the same. The depiction of the chapel and council chamber is also very clear. The men on the barge in the foreground are preparing to pass under the bridge, taking down the mast.

though Christiaan Huygens claimed to have solved the problem in 1646 and Robert Hooke, who assisted Wren in the design of St Paul's Cathedral, demonstrated the application of the arc in 1671. (The inner dome of St Paul's, completed in 1711, does appear to conform to a catenary.) It is unlikely that the architects of Ouse Bridge understood clearly what a catenary was in 1565, though they must have been familiar with arch construction in general, and it is possible that, knowing the span and height required they achieved the design by rule of thumb. However, a study of the measurements of the arch reveals that a slippage of a mere one or two feet could turn a semicircle into something approaching a catenary (J. Taylor, pers. comm.; Jardine 1999, 71–6, 332–4; Maor 1994, 140–6). Certainly, further repairs were undertaken in 1571 and 1572, and it has been suggested that the ban on coal and timber wagons or those with iron-bound wheels crossing the bridge indicate the

corporation's anxiety about its construction. The prohibition of heavy or iron-bound wagons was of long standing, however, and applied to paved streets as well as bridges, since they caused damage to the road surface. It was not uncommon for bridge arches to settle once the centring had been removed, without affecting the safety of the structure (see Fig.15). Undermining by the current ('scouring') or by collision were much more common, and the corporation's concern may have been not so much fear of structural fault in the new bridge as an all-too-vivid memory of the collapse of the old (Davies 1880, 201; *YCR* **6**, 151; **7**, 49; Cook 1998, 49–50). Unfortunately, artistic representations of the bridge are not sufficiently detailed to indicate whether there had been any shift in the voussoirs of the arch, while variations in the shape of the arch itself probably tell us more about problems faced by the artist than about his subject.

Ouse-bridge at York.

Fig.40 *(above; no.111) This stylised view of the bridge from downstream by Toms (1736) shows the shape of the arches but not in proportion to each other. It shows timber-framed houses hanging over the central arch and other buildings on the outer arches. These buildings were probably shops and residential accommodation. On the left is the prison with the chapel behind it.*

Fig.41 *(below; no.147) This engraving by Cave shows the east end of the chapel, dating from the 13th century. It also shows the steep rise of the bridge to the centre. The drawing for this was probably done in 1809 and it may be that the top surface of the road has been removed on the north side (at right). Beyond the bridge is Micklegate with the tower of St Martin-cum-Gregory on the left.*

Fig.42 (no.78) *This watercolour by Thomas White (1802) is a wonderful depiction of activity on King's Staith, a cargo of thatching reeds or straw having been unloaded from a sailing barge, with a horse-drawn cart waiting to be loaded. Two unhitched carts are waiting on the far right. The steep slope down to the river in the foreground is still evident today. The height of the central arch of the bridge may have been exaggerated in relation to its width, emphasising the steepness of the road. A mail coach is crossing the bridge, the driver blowing his post horn. The Guildhall can be seen through the central arch and a barge is coming under the bridge, having lowered its mast. The 'scar' on the bridge where buildings had once been can clearly be seen to the right of the central arch; grass is now growing on the masonry.*

Whether shaped by accident or design, the new bridge proved durable and elegant, serving the city for almost 250 years. The four pointed, or Gothic, arches were basically those of the medieval bridge strengthened and improved, those nearest the bank standing over dry land, at least when the river level was low. Over these the medieval buildings remained, notably St William's Chapel and the council chamber, though some repair and rebuilding had proved necessary. Small houses and shops were built at each end of the narrower central arch and let, mainly to leather workers, providing rents for the maintenance of the bridge, though not at the rate initially hoped for. These are clearly depicted in the views by Francis Place (c.1703) and by W.H. Toms (1736) (Figs.38 and 40). In 1745 it was ordered that they should be taken down; some rebuilding seems to have been planned, but in 1764, three houses were removed from the south side.

A plan by Dr White in 1782 (Fig.22, p.34) shows those that remained, but more houses were taken down in 1793, leaving the central arch clear. The narrowness of the road (about 16ft wide, plus a footpath on the south side) posed few problems to traffic, but the steep rise over the arch made for difficulties in adverse conditions. The city authorities soon ordered that the road surface be sanded, and Raine refers to a horse having been kept at the approach to aid carts making the ascent (Raine 1955, 222). The incline is best shown in Cave's view of the east end of the chapel (Fig.41) and by the angle of the coaches which 18th-century artists loved to show crossing the bridge (for example, Fig.42), though the roadway must have looked alarmingly steep and narrow to the outside passengers.

The bridge was much admired. William Camden, in 1586, thought it 'the largest arch I have ever seen'

Fig.43 *Elevations of the Ouse Bridge in York and the Rialto Bridge in Venice with measurements. This undated illustration is by an as yet unidentified artist (Evelyn Collection 161, YAYAS, Minster Library)*

Fig.44 *Modern photograph of corbels from the old Ouse Bridge, re-set into the wall of a warehouse next to the King's Arms on King's Staith. The Royal Commission calls them '13th-century shaped stone brackets', probably on the grounds that there was a house nearby in the 13th century (RCHMY 5, 104). Hutchinson and Palliser (1980) merely call them 'amorphous medieval corbels'. They do, however, closely resemble the corbels depicted on many views of the old bridge (see Figs.24, 42, 65, 72) and it is eminently possible that they were incorporated in a nearby building when the bridge was demolished early in the 19th century.*

(Palliser and Palliser 1979, 11), though he got his figures wrong; John Evelyn in 1654 said 'The Middle Arch [is] larger than any I have seene in all England.' (ibid., 20). Other visitors compared it to Antonio da Ponte's Rialto Bridge in Venice (Fig.43), which it was thought to exceed in width by a very satisfying seven feet — 'though I think not', wrote Daniel Defoe, and sadly he appears to have been right (ibid., 33). The removal of houses from the bridge in the course of the 18th century revealed the stepped facing of pale limestone, originally devised to increase the width of the roadway, which, with the supporting corbels, now emphasised the elegant sweep of the arch (Figs.42 and 65). Several of these corbels, much weathered, can still be seen built into the wall of the King's Staith (D. Tweddle, pers. comm.; see Fig.44). The whole ensemble 'composes a scene that would have delighted Canaletti, and rivals many of his finest Venetian views' (Edward Dayes, quoted in Murray et. al. 1990, 6). John Carter was ecstatic about it (see p.65). The scene proved a magnet for visiting artists,

notably William Marlow, Joseph Farington, Thomas Girtin, John Varley and John Sell Cotman. J.M.W. Turner produced lively preliminary sketches in 1797 but unfortunately he never turned them into completed paintings. Amongst the local artists, Joseph Halfpenny and Henry Cave were perhaps the most useful as they aimed to record the buildings with accuracy. Antiquarian interest in the old bridge remained long after its removal in 1810–20. A print, based on a sketch by John Carter, appeared in Britton's *Picturesque Antiquities of English Cities* in 1828, and even at the end of the century, Ridsdale Tate was producing reconstructions as greetings cards, based on Halfpenny (1807) and Cave (1813). York Public Library was selling copies of Tate's cards as Christmas cards as late as the year 2000. A stylised view of the bridge can be seen in the Guildhall west window, designed and painted in 1960 by H.W. Harvey (Fig.45). So, as late as the second half of the 20th century old Ouse Bridge still featured in the art of York.

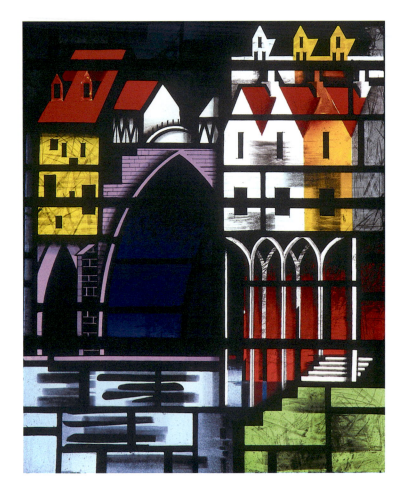

Fig.45 (no.113) *Each of the five lights of the west window in the Guildhall illustrates a particular aspect of York life. This is a detail from the fourth light which illustrates commerce. It is a stylised view of the bridge with all the buildings it once supported. As late as 1960, when this glass was installed, the old Ouse Bridge still featured in the art of York.*

Ouse Bridge, 1810 onwards

In 1795 Ouse Bridge was in need of repair (see, for example, Fig.46). It was also too narrow and the rise and fall over the arch were too steep, causing considerable delay to traffic within the city and between the east and west parts of the county. A proposal to replace it with a single-span iron bridge came to nothing, and in 1808 the decision was taken to widen the existing bridge, at an estimated cost of £60,000 over a ten-year time-span. A further proposal, to raise the sum by a toll on foot passengers, was soon abandoned, and instead £8,000 was raised by public subscription. It was hoped that this and the existing horse and carriage toll would cover the cost in 21 years. A competition to find the best design for the scheme was held, the assessor being Thomas Harrison, an experienced bridge designer with a practice in Chester. The first prize was awarded to architect Peter Atkinson jr., from the York practice originally started by John Carr. An Act of Parliament was obtained, but a survey by Harrison revealed that the structure of the bridge was in such disrepair that a complete rebuilding would be necessary. His report, produced in February 1810, gives further details.

The large arch, and the adjoining ones to the east are . . . in a tolerable state of repair; the remaining three arches are ruinous, and unfit to remain or be connected with any new work. The breakwaters and spandrils of the arches on the south side are shattered in several places.

Fig.46   (no.95) This unusual view by an unknown artist in around 1809 shows the remains of a cutwater and the easternmost arch of the bridge from the north side after demolition work had started. It shows clearly how dilapidated the bridge was by this date. Stone rubble can be seen on the bank.

CAVE. LOW OUSEGATE.

WORKMEN PULLING DOWN THE HOUSES FOR THE BRIDGE IMPROVEMENT.

Fig.47 (no.166) This is Ridsdale Tate's tracing from Cave's drawing (1809 or 1810) of workmen pulling down houses for the bridge improvement. The church tower is that of St Michael Spurriergate, before it was reduced in height. The houses and shops which stood on the north side of Low Ousegate, in front of the church, are also shown (see Fig.78); these were demolished to allow the road over the bridge to be widened. The same thing happened on the other side of the bridge in Bridge Street, at the bottom of Micklegate.

Widening the bridge and raising the road at each end would 'cause an unnecessary thickness and weight of materials upon the side arches', and thus the stonework would take up too great a proportion of the waterway, restricting the flow of the river and the passage of vessels.

The present bridge . . . will completely change its ancient character and picturesque appearance, and nothing will remain but the large distorted arch, with the Gothic or pointed arches at the sides . . . [The] great and unnecessary bulk of the piers . . . will appear as deformities proper to be removed, than as beauties in any way desirable to be retained (Thomas Harrison, Report, WYAS, HE/50; *York Courant*, 5 March 1810).

His further comment that building a new bridge would cost no more, and possibly less, than repairing the old one convinced the council. The Act was amended, Peter Atkinson was appointed as architect, the building contract went to Hiram Craven of Oakworth near Keighley, and soon houses were being taken down to widen and raise the approaches from Low Ousegate and Bridge Street (see Fig.47).

The impending loss of the old bridge and its buildings naturally aroused controversy. York had lost much of its attraction as a social resort for the gentry without as yet gaining from industrial development, and it was regarded as rather dowdy. The corporation hoped to create a more spacious and elegant city by removing the city walls and improving lines of communication between its remaining attractions. Conservationists, however, deplored the threat to the city's ancient buildings and though the walls and bars had been saved — for the time being — they now saw the bridge in danger. Visiting the city in 1806, the eminent and outspoken antiquary, John Carter, thundered his disapproval of the state of 'those condemned innocents, those suffering gemells of art, those chief jewels in the civic crown of York, Ouse Bridge and chapel, otherwise "nuisances"', incidentally providing future historians with a rare description of the chapel interior before adding his own interpretation of the corporation's motives.

The reasons urged for the approaching overthrow of the bridge is want of room thereon for the rapid dash of equestrians and barouche drivers, improving the ready communication between the city and the race-ground, the stand at one end and the drop at the other, and prevents the bringing about a scheme for a new street from Lounger's Corner in the cross ways, Conyng Street, to Mumper's bounds, outside Micklegate Bar.

The point had already been made, with a similar hint of venom, by Thomas Rowlandson, in 'York City during the Races' c.1800 (York City Art Gallery R1709; reproduced in RCHMY **3**, pl.162). Carter suggested an alternative route from the Minster via Stonegate

Fig.48 *(no.140) This sketch by Cave is valuable because it puts other pictures of the interior of the chapel into context. It is a general view of the west end showing the screen and also the first arch and part of the second along the north side of the central aisle. It shows a capital in situ, one element of which is on the ground in Fig.29. On the north wall is the blind arcade: pointed arches with simple chamfered moulding and shafts with simple bell-type capitals. On the left is part of the first arch of the south arcade but it seems to be blocked up to the level of the capital. Workmen are busy in the council chamber behind the chapel and a timber-framed building can be seen beyond that. There are large timber supports for strengthening, and it may well be that the chapel was built first and that the council chamber was later built on the exterior west wall. This picture shows the complexity of the inter-relationship between the buildings.*

Fig.49 *(left; no.91) This interesting wash drawing by Cave in the early 19th century shows an artist, possibly Cave himself, sketching the bridge. There is a boat half sunk in the mud and a mooring on a chain which would have enabled a boat to move up and down as the water level rose and fell.*

Fig.50 *(below; no.101) The bridge is very dilapidated in this painting by Cave, and demolition work has actually begun. At the far end of the bridge St William's Chapel has been removed, and most of the toll booth beside the main arch has gone. The debtors' gaol still stands on its extended arch. The buildings with timber shoring on the right were to disappear along with the rest of the bridge in 1817–18. Cave has depicted clearly the undersides of the arches and the timber framing beneath the house at the right. The round arch with a pointed arch behind it shows just how much the bridge had been altered over the centuries.*

Fig.51 *(no.163) Measured wash drawing by Peter Atkinson of the elevation of the proposed new bridge, as finally accepted in 1810. When the bridge was eventually built the elegant top balustrade and the niches between the arches were modified.*

past the Guildhall, crossing the river by a new bridge (at a point near the former Roman crossing), and thence by All Saints, North Street, to Micklegate Bar.

By this procedure Ouse Bridge and chapel may be preserved to the antiquary and man of constant habits, and become a bridle-way for old Remembrance and sure-footed Gratitude. As for the new bridge . . . the road may be made wide enough for Speculation and Folly, Dissipation and Want, to ride over abreast! J. C. (Gentleman's Magazine **76**, November 1806, 1187; Davies 1880, 202–4).

Artists hastened to depict the process of dilapidation, getting under the feet of the demolition men as they sketched the bridge, the chapel and even each other (Fig.49). 'The destroying hand of time, and a predominant spirit of improvement, are lessening the number, as well as the figure of the remaining antiquities of York; and the forms of many of them will be shortly known only in their engraved representations', wrote Henry Cave, making rapid sketches of the dwindling bridge and chapel, some reproduced as etchings in his *Antiquities of York* (Cave 1813,

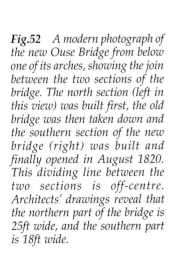

Fig.52 *A modern photograph of the new Ouse Bridge from below one of its arches, showing the join between the two sections of the bridge. The north section (left in this view) was built first, the old bridge was then taken down and the southern section of the new bridge (right) was built and finally opened in August 1820. This dividing line between the two sections is off-centre. Architects' drawings reveal that the northern part of the bridge is 25ft wide, and the southern part is 18ft wide.*

pls.XXIII–XXVII; see Figs.27–30, 41). Joseph Half-penny, who in 1799 had been a member of the corporation committee formed to consider the future of the city walls (Curr 1984, 27), had been able to produce more measured views of the bridge and chapel in 1807 (Halfpenny 1807, pls.21–3; see Figs.26, 39, 72). As the prime concern of both artists was to record the monuments as accurately as possible, their work is of considerable historical interest.

The new bridge, of brown limestone, was designed by Peter Atkinson in classical style (Fig.51), with three arches, the central arch having a span of 75ft and the side arches of 64ft (RCHMY 3, pls.143–4). At 43ft wide (north–south), it would be more than twice the width of the old bridge and it was to be built in two halves longitudinally, the north side first, so that the old bridge could continue in use until the new section was open to traffic. The join is still clearly visible from below the bridge (see Fig.52). The laying of the foundation stone in 1810 was delayed by a sudden rise in the river level until 10 December, when a procession of the corporation, freemasons and bridge constructors, with bands and banners, accompanied 'The *Stone*, weighing *two tons and a half*, on a rully [open-sided harvest wagon] drawn by three horses'; the stone was laid by the Lord Mayor, George Peacock, after which 'feasting and general rejoicing were kept up till a very late hour' (Hargrove 1818, 199–201). However, the enterprise soon incurred a debt of £30,000, leading to further delays. As in earlier years, the sheer scale of the undertaking had outrun the funds available. York was not alone in this: the Clifton Suspension Bridge in Bristol, admittedly a more ambitious scheme, begun in 1832, was also caught in mid-stream, as it were, and was only completed in 1864. At last in 1815 an Act of Parliament allowed the money to be obtained by rates levied on the three Ridings of Yorkshire, in five annual instalments of £6,000 (a sixth instalment to be added if necessary), as well as contributions from the City, the Ainsty, the Liberty of St Peter and the corporation,

Fig.53 *(no.167) Though no more than a rapid sketch, this is a rare and valuable view, showing the northern section of the new bridge with the old bridge still standing behind it. It is the only known picture which shows the old bridge alongside the new. The view is from the north, with a boat at right, the spire of All Saints North Street at far right and the tower of St Michael Spurriergate at left. There is no indication that Turner ever worked up this sketch into a finished painting.*

Fig.54 *(no.164) Portrait of Peter Atkinson, c.1820, holding his drawing of the new bridge which he gave to the Lord Mayor of York.*

Fig.55 *(no.164) Detail from Shee's portrait of Peter Atkinson showing the drawing of the new bridge over the River Ouse which he presented to George Peacock. The date on the drawing seems to be December 10th 1820. In fact, the foundation stone for the new bridge was laid by Peacock on December 10th 1810, but he was Lord Mayor of York again in August 1820 when the bridge was finally opened.*

amounting to £615 a year. Tolls on the bridge, some £3,000 a year, would continue only until the expenses of construction were paid off. Once complete, repairs to the bridge would be the sole responsibility of the corporation. A plan to cut costs by reducing the width of the bridge and replacing the balustrades with a plain parapet wall met with criticism from William Hargrove, editor and part-proprietor of the *York Herald*: 'To immure the bridge with close dead walls, in lieu of displaying open and elegant balustrades, will certainly but poorly compensate for the saving derived; whilst the contraction of the width . . . will betray a parsimonious disposition, rather than evince a prudent frugality'. For Britain's largest county, this was not good enough. Built to the original plan, the bridge would have 'stood through successive centuries, a monument of the scientific superiority, and enlightened liberality of the age in which we live' (Hargrove 1818, 205–6 and plate opposite p.197; RCHMY **3**, pls.142–4).

The financial problems solved, work could resume, and the northern half, completed in 1817, was formally opened by a procession of six Royal Mail coaches on 1 January 1818. Visiting the city in that year, J.M.W. Turner caught the moment in a rapid outline sketch of considerable interest, since it shows the new bridge with the remains of the old one still standing (Fig.53). The entire structure was completed in 1820 and officially opened on 19 August, by the same Lord Mayor, George Peacock, now in his second term of office. There was still more rejoicing when the toll was finally abolished on 18 June 1829 and drivers and passengers enjoyed the novelty of free passage across the Ouse. Contemporaries noted that the first toll-free vehicle was a cart carrying timber for more rebuilding, this time of the Minster after the fire started by Jonathan Martin in February of that year.

Fig.56 (no.168) *This is Cave's pencil drawing which compares the old (top) and new (bottom) bridge from the south (King's Staith). The top picture shows the buildings which had been demolished, including the chapel and debtors' gaol on the left, and houses on the right whose removal allowed the tower of St Martin-le-Grand in Coney Street to be seen in the bottom picture. The new bridge as finally built may be compared with Atkinson's original proposal (Fig.51) with its top balustrade.*

Illustrations

The River Ouse

1. *c. 1670   From the Old Waterhouse in York*

William Lodge. Etching.

View looking downstream, showing Lendal Tower, Ouse Bridge, St William's Chapel, All Saints North Street, North Street Postern and the chimneys of Buckingham House.

York City Art Gallery R4148, R5083, R5084; also R5082 (identified as ? after Lodge).

Minster Library: Revd Robert William Bilton Hornby Collection, York Antiquities vol.2 (Add. MS 320), 73.

Lendal Tower is shown with three storeys and in a ruinous state. After a failed attempt to provide a piped water supply for the city in 1616–32, it was used as a warehouse until 1677, when it became part of a new water supply scheme. Ouse Bridge and St William's Chapel have been drawn inaccurately and the shoreline is suspect. There is much activity on the river, the fishermen reflecting Lodge's own interests.

2. *c.1676   York from beyond the Water Tower at St Maryes*

Francis Place. Pen and ink with grey wash, some features tinted red-brown, on two conjoined sheets.

View looking downstream with St Mary's Tower in the foreground.

British Museum Department of Prints and Drawings 1850-2-23-834.

Also the same view:

York from St Mary's Water Tower (Fig.57)

Francis Place. Ink and wash.

4¾ x 9¾in. (121 x 245mm).

York City Art Gallery R1858.

YAT Collection TG17.

Also engravings of the same view:

York City Art Gallery R1859 (inscribed Lodge), reproduced in Drake 1736, 332.

York City Art Gallery R5081, R5085 (two copies, one annotated).

York City Art Gallery R5086, a wider view of the river.

Lodge and Place often worked together, sketching the same view, so precise attribution is not always possible.

Fig.57 (no.2) This shows St Mary's Tower in the foreground at left, with Lendal Tower (left) and North Street Tower (right) on the bend in the river, where Lendal Bridge is today. It shows clearly the Guildhall beyond, and the river wall with its entrances to the water lanes. It also shows the sharp bend in the river and open fields on the right (where the Royal Mail sorting office now stands). In the foreground at right is a small sailing barge carrying timber or reeds.

3. *c.1680 The Ouse at Lendal Ferry*

Francis Place. Engraving.

View looking upstream, with North Street Postern on the left and Lendal Tower on the right.

Reproduced in Drake 1736, 331.

Tracing in 'Old York Sketches, Tracings etc., chiefly by Edwin Ridsdale Tate, collected by George Benson', p.86 (York Public Library).

Also the same view:

Near the Manor Shore, York (Fig.9, p.14)

William Lodge. Engraving.

York City Art Gallery R1977.

4. *1703 York from near the Confluence of the Rivers Ouse and Foss* (also listed as 'York, as you go to Water Foulford') (Fig.1, p.3)

Francis Place. Pencil, brown wash and sepia ink.

7¼ x 12¾in. (180 x 323mm).

View looking north.

York City Art Gallery R1978.

YAT Collection TG18.

Reproduced in Benson 1919, 121, and Murray et al. 1990, pl.119.

Engraving in Drake 1736, 303.

5. *c.1706 Panoramic View of York Castle and Surrounding Countryside*

Francis Place. Ink drawing with watercolour, on conjoined sheets.

View looking south from Clifford's Tower.

British Museum Department of Prints and Drawings 1850-2-23-838 (LB 38).

YAT Collection II 6 9.

The right-hand side shows the river meandering towards Fulford. St George's Fields has linen bleaching and a sand-pit, and there is a half-built boat on the stocks on the west bank of the Ouse.

6. *1736 York, its boundarys, the peculiar districk, Aynsty, belonging to it; the course of the river Ouse; the proposed cuts to be made in it for bettering its navigation; with a draught of the grand project for cutting a Canal from the Humber to the City anno. 1616* (Fig.3, p.6)

Double-page map showing the course of the river from the confluence of the Swale and Ure near Aldborough to the Humber and the proposed canal from Fulford to Broomfleet.

Reproduced in Drake 1736, 380–1.

The original map may have been made in 1616, when John Hart was sent (with a map) to seek advice in Holland (*YCHB* **34**, fo.102), though there is a reference to a plan of the river being prepared in May 1603 after James I agreed to support improvements; that plan, showing a new cut to shorten the river, was referred to on 15 January 1603/4 (*YCHB* **32**, fo.309). A plan of the

proposed canal based on that in Drake is in Duckham 1967, 45. Duckham says that Drake's version is rather fanciful.

7. *1736 A South-West View of the City of York* (Fig.2, p.4)

William Henry Toms, after Peter Monamy. Etching and engraving.

11¾ x 14¾in. (302 x 379mm).

View looking north-west along the river, from the confluence of the Ouse and Foss to Ouse Bridge.

York City Art Gallery R3159.

Reproduced in Drake 1736, 249, and in Murray et al. 1990, pl.118.

Monamy may not have drawn this on the spot, but worked it up from a rough drawing sent to him by Drake.

See also:

1751 A View of the City of York from the River Ouse/ Une Vue de la Ville de York depuis la Riviere Ouse

William Henry Toms, after Chatelain. Hand-coloured engraving.

Very similar to the previous view.

York City Art Gallery R1778.

8. *1756 Prospect of a Noble Terras Walk* (Fig.12, p.18)

Nathan Drake, engraved by Charles Grignion. Etching and engraving.

17½ x 24in. (446 x 610mm).

View looking north along the New Walk.

York City Art Gallery R2510.

Reproduced in Murray et al. 1990, pl.120.

Evelyn Collection 29 (YAYAS, Minster Library).

YAT Collection TG24.

Shows the river with sailing barges and with both banks visible on the left. Ouse Bridge is in the background.

9. *1789 Tower at Lendal End*

Joseph Halfpenny. Drawing with grey wash.

View down the river from opposite the Manor Shore. Probably a preliminary sketch, with no great detail.

Wakefield Art Gallery, Gott Collection 1789/2/15.

10. *c.1797 York Minster from the Ouse, near St Mary's Abbey*

Thomas Girtin. Watercolour.

13½ x 19¼in. (340 x 489mm).

View across the river, with sailing barge full of coal or grain being unloaded at St Mary's Landing. The Abbey, Marygate Tower, the hospitium and the Minster can all be seen behind.

Harewood House Trust.

Reproduced in colour in Hill 1999, pl.36.

Fig.58 (no.11) *Looking upstream, across to the New Walk from the west bank. The trees have filled out since 1736 (see Fig.2, p.4). Ouse Bridge, the chapel, the staith and the buildings of the city can all be seen in the background.*
[*The New Walk, York, c.1798 (pencil and watercolour on paper) by Thomas Girtin (1775–1802). Yale Center for British Art, Paul Mellon Collection, USA. Photo: Bridgeman Art Library.*]

11. c.1798 *The New Walk, York* (Fig.58)

Thomas Girtin. Watercolour over pencil with body-colour on textured laid paper.

12¼ x 21¾in. (313 x 555mm).

View looking upstream and across the river from the west bank. Ouse Bridge and King's Staith are in the background, New Walk at centre right.

Yale Center for British Art (Paul Mellon Collection) B1977.14.4906 (i).

Reproduced in black and white in Morris 1986, 67, pl.64.

12. n.d. (c.1800) *Waterworks and Ouse Bridge*

John Claude Nattes. Pen and ink/mezzotint.

View downstream from Lendal Tower.

York City Art Gallery R2936.

Useful for its depiction of the waterworks.

13. c.1800 *General View of York from Opposite the New Walk Terrace*

John Claude Nattes. Pen and ink drawing.

View from beside Skeldergate ferry, showing the postern. Ouse Bridge is in the background.

York City Art Gallery R2932.

See also no.52d.

14. c.1800 *On the River Ouse, looking upstream* (Fig.59)

Henry Cave. Pencil.

9 x 13¼in. (233 x 338mm).

View from the east bank of the river just north of the Guildhall, looking towards Lendal Tower, with some detail of buildings on the west bank.

York City Art Gallery R3167.

Reproduced in Murray et al. 1990, pl.58.

15. c.1803 *River Ouse*

Henry Cave. Pencil.

General view looking north from the west bank.

York City Art Gallery R3052.

See also Evelyn Collection 158 (YAYAS, Minster Library).

16. c.1803 *River Ouse*

Henry Cave. Pencil.

General view looking north from the east bank.

York City Art Gallery R3054.

17. n.d. *River Ouse from Skeldergate Postern*

Henry Cave. Pencil and watercolour.

General view upstream.

York City Art Gallery R19.

Fig.59 *(no.14) This is a view of the River Ouse from the east bank, looking towards Lendal Tower. The waterworks are on the right and St Olave's can also be seen, looking rather squat. There is a jetty at left and a loading support at roof level, confirming the river's use for trade. Fishing is also taking place, and the bucket and barrel suggest that water was collected from the river.*

18. *1804   River Ouse*

John Varley. Watercolour.

View upstream from near North Street Postern with a sailing barge and small fishing boat. The lack of detailed representation of the buildings makes this useful only as a general view.

York City Art Gallery R264.

19. *1808   Ouze Bridge*

J. Storer, after Dayes. Engraving.

View from the north showing industrial buildings on the river bank on the right.

York City Art Gallery R4520.2.

20. *1815   York from below Ouse Bridge* (Fig.60)

Paul Sandby Munn. Watercolour.

View from the west bank of the river, south of the bridge.

York City Art Gallery R217.

Also preliminary monochrome sketch of 1804, R227.

21. *1826   York from opposite the Manor Shore*

John Varley. Watercolour.

View looking across the river to the Minster, with the (present) Museum Gardens, Multangular Tower, Lendal Tower and North Street Postern. This is a highly finished painting in bright colours, probably based on a sketch of c.1803.

York City Art Gallery R379.

22. *1826   View on the Ouse near York*

Henry Gastineau. Watercolour and bodycolour.

7¼ x 10¼in. (186 x 262mm).

Looking downstream from St Mary's Tower, where a boat is being unloaded. A very atmospheric picture but no great detail.

York City Art Gallery R1553.

23. *n.d.   View up the River*

Thomas Shotter Boys. Lithograph with ochre wash.

Contrary to the title of the picture, this is a view looking downstream, with the Guildhall and river frontage each side.

Minster Library: Revd Robert William Bilton Hornby Collection, York Antiquities vol.2 (Add. MS 320), 85. Also YK38.

24. *1834   River Ouse. Longitudinal Section for Ten Miles from Rawcliffe Lane to Moreby Landing. Inscribed Thomas Rhodes, Engineer, 18th Jan. 1834*

Drawn by H. Renton, redrawn by George Benson.

Plan of the river, showing depths at summer water level and widths at Ouse Bridge, New Walk, Fulford Landing, Bishopthorpe Palace, above and below Naburn ferry, and at Moreby Landing. Details of the proposed new lock at Naburn are also given.

Reproduced in Benson 1925 (fig.25).

25. *1836   Old Towers at Northstreet Postern, Lendal and Marygate Landing* (Fig.61)

Henry Brown. Wood engraving.

3½ x 5¾in. (90 x 145mm).

A lively view upstream from below Lendal ferry.

Brown and Brown 1836 (plates not numbered).

26. *1836   View from the Tower at Marygate Landing* (Fig.11, p.16)

Henry Brown. Wood engraving.

3½ x 5¾in. (90 x 145mm).

View looking downstream.

A somewhat stylised representation.

Brown and Brown 1836 (plates not numbered).

27. *1836   The Boat Yard, Manor Shore* (Fig.6, p.10)

Henry Brown. Wood engraving.

2¾ x 4½in. (67 x 113 mm).

View of the east shore with small pleasure boats, some drawn up on the shore, others being rowed on the water. Behind is part of the Abbey and Yorkshire Museum.

Brown and Brown 1836 (plates not numbered).

Fig.60   (no.20) View from the west bank, south of the bridge. It shows the rise up the river bank, and Ouse Bridge, St Michael Spurriergate and the Minster in the background. In fact the old Ouse Bridge had gone by 1815 when this was painted and it is known that the preliminary sketch for this watercolour was produced in 1804. There is a keel with a sail and several moored rowing boats.

Fig.61 *(no.25) This engraving shows the ferry crossing from Lendal to North Street Postern, along with the hospitium and precinct wall of St Mary's Abbey. The cows drinking, man fishing, two dogs and small sailing boats all add life to the picture.*

28. *1840   St Mary's Abbey, York: the Abbey Grounds*

John Skinner Prout. Lithograph.

View from across the river, showing the shoreline, with the hospitium and abbey gatehouse (c.1500) behind, and a sailing barge being drawn up by the shore.

Prout 1840, pl.9.

Minster Library YK360.

29. *1840   From the Manor Shore, York*

John Skinner Prout. Lithograph.

Looking downstream and across the river, with Lendal Tower, the Guildhall and North Street Postern. A family is enjoying a picnic on the river bank in the foreground.

Prout 1840, pl.11.

30. *1845   King's Staith, July 1845*

W.H. Fox Talbot. Photograph.

View looking directly across the river from Queen's Staith.

London, Science Museum, 360/69.

Reproduced in Murray 1986, 19.

The river frontage from Ouse Bridge to Cumberland House. This house was built c.1710 and its doorway is

at the side, in Cumberland Street, because of the danger of flooding. Cumberland Street was originally known as Thursgail, in c.1560 became Middle Water Lane, gaining its present name in 1880. First Water Lane (now King Street) is in the centre of this picture and the double-gabled building to its right was removed in 1851. To the left of the lane is the building which is now the King's Arms. The central doorway seen in the photograph was replaced in 1898 by a side door, probably to allow access during floods.

31. *1852   Tower at Lendal Ferry (east side) taken 8 October 1852* (Fig.10, p.15)

William Pumphrey. Photograph.

View from the south-east.

Pumphrey 1853, pl.5 (portfolio in York Public Library).

Evelyn Collection 423 (YAYAS, Minster Library).

Reproduced in Murray 1986, 26.

32. *1852   The Guildhall, York, 20 April 1852*

George Fowler Jones. Photograph.

The river frontage from Lendal to south of St Martin Coney Street, with Common Hall Lane and its staith.

Reproduced in Murray 1986, 76.

33. *1853 River Ouse, York*

George Fowler Jones. Photograph.

The river frontage from Lendal Tower to north of Ouse Bridge.

Reproduced in Murray 1986, 75.

This view from the Manor Shore (now The Esplanade) shows the 16th-century river wall, with lanes leading from landing places to Coney Street. Ten years after this photograph was taken, Lendal Bridge was opened.

34. *1853 King's Staith etc.*

William Pumphrey. Photograph.

View from the west bank of the river.

Pumphrey 1853, pl.56 (portfolio in York Public Library).

Reproduced in Murray 1986, 40.

King's Staith was raised and repaved in 1774, and rebuilt again in 1820. There were steps leading down to the staith from the old bridge, which were replaced in 1810–20. By this time First Water Lane and the twingabled house shown in no.30 have been cleared. The houses on the right were taken down in 1882 when the clearance of the water lanes was completed.

35. *1854 Lendall Ferry*

Roger Fenton. Photograph (published 1 October 1854).

View looking downstream from the steps of the ferry landing on the west bank of the river. There are working boats in the foreground and rowing boats moored at Hill's boatyard beside the Guildhall.

Reproduced in Murray 1986, 44.

Also in Willis 1973 (no page number).

36. *1858 Bird's-Eye View of the City of York* (Fig.8, pp.12–13)

Nathaniel Whittock. Lithograph (J. Storey).

21 x 36in. (533 x 916mm).

River Ouse and river frontages from Scarborough Bridge to the New Walk.

York City Art Gallery R1946.

YAT Collection TG31.

Reproduced in colour as a foldout in Murray 1988.

This shows clear detail of the river walls, walks, wharves and boatyard, industrial buildings, Scarborough Bridge and embankment, Ouse Bridge, Lendal and Skeldergate ferries. On the river are Humber keels, lighters, skiffs, ferry boats and a paddle steamer.

37. *1865 York from the New Walk* (Fig.62)

William Boddy. Watercolour.

Fig.62 *(no.37) This fine watercolour by William Boddy shows the New Walk, looking towards Queen's Staith and the new (1810) Ouse Bridge in the background.*

77

View across the river and upstream to Ouse Bridge, with good detail of both banks.
York City Art Gallery R3305.

38. *1866   York from Skeldergate Ferry*
John Bell. Oil on canvas.
24½ x 36½in. (635 x 915mm).
View looking upstream showing the New Walk on the right and part of the river bank on the left, with barges moored.
York City Art Gallery 487.

39. *c.1875   York from Scarborough Railway Bridge*
John Bell. Oil on canvas.
River banks from Marygate to the Guildhall, with Lendal Bridge, viewed from the east end of Scarborough Bridge.
York City Art Gallery 484.

40. *n.d.   The King's Staith, York (houses standing in the 19th century)*
C.H. Simpson. Pencil drawing on an envelope.
On the reverse of the drawing is inscribed: 'Taken from his garden at the back of the house. Seen across the river'.
York City Art Gallery R2405.
A small but quite detailed view of buildings on the staith, many of which were demolished in the 1880s, starting with the Dutch-gabled one on the right.

41. *1885   Old House on the King's Staith*
J. England Jefferson. Photomechanical reproduction of a pen and ink drawing.
The Ouse Bridge Inn, with the east end of the bridge on the left and the corner of King Street on the right.
Benson and Jefferson 1886, pl.39.
The 17th-century inn, formerly the King's Arms, was much altered in 1898 and again in 1973–4, when it also reverted to its old name. The thick ground-floor walls on the south and west were probably built because of the risk of flooding.

42. *1885   Working barges*
Photograph.
These barges are on the River Foss at Castle Mills Bridge, but the photograph shows the type of local river traffic which would have been using the Ouse towards the end of the 19th century.
Reproduced in Law 1989.

43. *1880–90   Ferry crossing at Howden Dyke*
Photograph.
This is not a York view but it is valuable in showing the type of ferry which would have crossed the Ouse

at Lendal, Skeldergate, and from Bridge Street to Low Ousegate when Ouse Bridge was out of action (for example in 1565; see p.55). The ferry boat is remarkably small to be carrying a loaded waggon and a horse, as well as four men.
Reproduced in Duckham 1967, fig.26.

44. *1891   The Yorkshire Ouse* (Fig.5, facing p.8)
Tom Bradley. Print from an ink drawing.
Pictorial strip-map of the river from Beningborough to Cawood.
Foldout in Bradley 1891.
Shows road and rail bridges, ferries and Naburn lock.

45. *1895   Skating on the River Ouse, February 1895*
Photograph.
View looking downstream from Ouse Bridge towards Skeldergate Bridge.
Reproduced in Law 1989.
Skaters and working boats. Clear view of revetments and landing places on the east side of the river.

46. *1895   Skating on the River Ouse, February 1895*
Photograph.
View looking downstream towards Lendal Bridge.
Reproduced in Willis 1973 (no page number).

47. *1896   The King's Staith, York*
William Boddy. Watercolour.
View from the bottom of Friargate. This street was originally named Hertergate, but from c.1560 it was known as Far Water Lane, being given its present name in 1808.
York City Art Gallery R2748.

48. *1903   The River Ouse at Skeldergate Bridge*
Photograph.
View looking upstream towards the bridge, with barges moored at the staith on the left. On the right is part of the New Walk, with Crimean War cannon.
Reproduced in Law 1989.

49. *1904   View up river from Skeldergate Ferry as it appeared about 200 years ago, 28th Feb. 1904* (Fig.14, p.20)
Edwin Ridsdale Tate. Pencil drawing.
Conjectural reconstruction of the south-west bank of the river and the buildings between Skeldergate ferry and Queen's Staith.
York City Art Gallery R5442.

50. *1910   River Ouse at low tide in 1910*
Photograph.
View downstream from Ouse Bridge to Skeldergate Bridge (cf. no.45).

Fig.63 (no.51) Section of Ridsdale Tate's 'York in the Fifteenth Century', showing the bridge, river and waterfronts. His conjectural reconstruction shows the staiths used by St Mary's Abbey, the Augustinians and the Franciscans. It also shows the city defences and two castle mottes, one each side of the river.

Reproduced in Law 1989.

Working boats, rowing boats and landing stages are seen at low water (rather than low tide, as the river was by this time no longer tidal).

51. *1914   York in the Fifteenth Century* (Fig.63; see also Fig.19, p.31)

Edwin Ridsdale Tate. Pencil, watercolour, and pen and black ink. Dated 15 May 1914.

19¾ x 42¾in. (505 x 1085mm).

Conjectural bird's-eye view looking north across the city from above Clementhorpe.

Mansion House, York.

Reproduced in Murray et al. 1990, pl.114.

Shows the course of the river through the city, with some detail of banks and river walls. The conjectural medieval bridge (c.1170–1565) is in the centre.

52. *n.d.   Drawings and Tracings from 'Old York Sketches, Tracings etc., chiefly by Edwin Ridsdale Tate, collected by George Benson' (York Public Library)*

a) *View up the Ouse from Hargrove's Library, from water-colour drawing lent by Mr George Benson*

Edwin Ridsdale Tate. Tracing.

No.236, p.90.

Hargrove's Library was in Coney Street.

b) *Old Ouse Bridge (1803) from Pencil Drawing by H. Cave, 1803 (lent by the Dean and Chapter of York)*

Edwin Ridsdale Tate. Ink drawing.

No.468, p.94.

c) *North Street Postern and Lendal Ferry, from ink wash drawing by J. Browne* (Fig.4, p.7)

Edwin Ridsdale Tate. Ink drawing.

No.543, p.90.

View from upstream, with ferry being fastened up and passenger waiting.

d) *(dated 1905) General View of York from opposite the New Walk (Skeldergate Postern and Ferry) from a pen and ink sketch by J.C. Nattes (lent by Dr W.A. Evelyn)*

Edwin Ridsdale Tate. Ink drawing.

No.590, p.94.

See also no.13.

e) *Waterworks, Ouse Bridge and York from a pen and ink sketch by J.C. Nattes (lent by Dr W.A. Evelyn)* (Fig.64)

Edwin Ridsdale Tate. Tracing.

No.591, p.93.

Lendal Tower and waterworks buildings from the east bank of the river, upstream. See also no.12.

Fig.64 *(no.52e) This is a very clear view of Lendal Tower and the waterworks buildings. It also shows the industrial buildings on the right (west) bank of the river, seldom depicted.*

f) *Mary Gate, York, 1881*

Edwin Ridsdale Tate. Unfinished pencil sketch.

On the back page.

Marygate Landing, with a barge; the south side of Marygate; the tower of St Olave's; the swimming baths (named); the hospitium; and the towers of the Minster and St Wilfrid's, from across the river.

53. *1933   River Ouse, 1933, Showing Lendal Bridge in the distance*

Photograph.

View looking upstream with embankments and warehouses.

Reproduced in Law 1989.

54. *1942   The Ouse from the Guildhall*

Henry Rushbury. Pencil, watercolour and black crayon. 15¼ x 18¾in. (385 x 473mm).

View from beside the Guildhall looking south towards Ouse Bridge, with barges, warehouses and industrial buildings on the west bank.

York City Art Gallery R2724.

Reproduced in colour in Murray et al. 1990, pl.66.

55. *n.d.   King's Staith and Far Water Lane*

Elizabeth Barstow. Watercolour.

Cobbled staith, gable end of a three-storey brick and timber house with a carved stone embedded in the wall. Timber jettied building on the right. Far Water Lane was renamed Friargate in 1808.

York City Art Gallery R9.

Ouse Bridge, 1154 and c.1170–1565

56. *n.d. (late 15th–early 16th century)   Alabaster carving, probably part of an altar reredos, showing the collapse of Ouse Bridge in 1154* (Fig.18, p.30)

One of four panels illustrating the life of St William found in Peasholme Green in 1957 on the site of the Holy Priests' House, and probably from the church of All Saints, Peasholme Green.

Now in the Yorkshire Museum.

Photograph in Willmot 1957, 36, fig.12.

57. *c.1414   Stained glass panel depicting the collapse of Ouse Bridge in 1154* (back cover)

The St William Window (nVII), York Minster, Panel 9c.

0.75 x 0.83m.

Probably by John Thornton of Coventry.

Date 1414 according to French 1999, 18–21. The window was previously assigned the date c.1423.

The medieval stone bridge is also shown in Panel 22c of the same window (reproduced in French 1999, 102).

St William crossing the bridge over the Ouse. The bridge is shown as stone with three arches and two rounded corbelled projections over the piers; in 1154, however, the date of the event being depicted, the bridge was still a timber construction. This is the occasion of the miracle of Ouse Bridge when William's presence ensured that none of the people who fell into the river when the bridge collapsed were drowned.

58. *Other windows in York Minster, now somewhat fragmented*:

a) North choir aisle, second from west, n9, right light, second panel from top.

b) Bellfounders' window, n24, three lights in upper row.

c) South aisle, second from west (reconstructed), s34, central light, upper row.

d) Chapter House, northern window, CH n3, upper row, left-hand panel (Toy 1985).

59. *1863–4   Window by William Wailes, showing the fall of Ouse Bridge in 1154*

St Wilfrid's Church, Duncombe Place, south aisle, third window from east, panel in tracery. The broken timber bridge and its relationship to the surface of the river may well be reasonably accurate, but the archbishop's vestments and the west end of York Minster are firmly set in the 19th century.

Other views of the medieval bridge are modern reconstructions:

See no.51, Fig.19, p.31.

60. *n.d.   Conjectural drawings of medieval Ouse Bridge*

(above) Elevations of buildings on the south side of the bridge, seen from the south.

(below) Elevations of buildings on the north side of bridge, also seen from the south.

Six arches of the bridge are shown.

Reproduced in Murray 2000, 3.

Original in author's collection.

Ouse Bridge, 1565–1810

61. *1700   York. The Ouse Bridge*

Francis Place. Pen and ink with grey wash.

Shows the central and two westernmost arches with St William's Chapel, north side, from the west bank of the river.

British Museum Department of Prints and Drawings 1850-2-23-840 (LB7).

Evelyn Collection 92 (YAYAS, Minster Library).

Reproduced in Croft-Murray and Hulton 1960, pl.252.

This is merely a preliminary sketch, but it shows some details not in no.63. The artist has written a note to himself below the central arch, saying 'bring the arch lower'.

62. *n.d. (c.1700)   Ouse Bridge from the North Side*

Francis Place. Wash drawing (roundel).

Looking through the central arch, with some detail of buildings on the west bank of the river below the bridge.

York City Art Gallery R1950.

Evelyn Collection 26 (YAYAS, Minster Library).

63. *1703   Ous Bridg York 1703* (Fig.38, p.56)

Francis Place. Pen and brown ink with washes of brown and grey, on two conjoined sheets.

4½ x 11½in. (117 x 296mm).

View from the north side. Inscribed 'Between the Butments or first spring of the Arch 83½ feet'.

British Museum Department of Prints and Drawings 1850-2-23-839 (LB6).

Evelyn Collection 830 (YAYAS, Minster Library).

See also: *1709 Old Ouse Bridge, York* (after pen and wash drawing by F. Place, 1709)

J. Beckett. Etching with surface tone.

View as above.

York City Art Gallery R5088.

64. *1760   Ouse Bridge, York*

I. Peake. Engraving.

Dated May 1st 1772, but the original drawing is said to have been made in 1760.

View from the south.

York City Art Gallery R4521 and R4523.

Minster Library YK234.

Later edition 'Published 1st July 1784 by S. Hooper'.

Also 1784 edition, inscribed 'from the Lady's Magazine'.

York City Art Gallery R4524 and R4525.

Minster Library YK228.

65. *c.1763   Ouse Bridge, York* (Fig.37, p.55; front cover)

William Marlow. Oil on canvas.

21 x 30¼in. (535 x 770mm).

View from the south, with buildings on both banks of the river as well as the bridge.

York City Art Gallery 176.

66. *n.d.   Chapel, St John's and Ouse Bridge*

Artist unknown. Wash drawing.

A very similar view to no.65.

Wakefield Art Gallery, Gott Collection 3/27.

67. *1783   The Old Ouse Bridge, York* (Fig.65)

Joseph Farington. Pen and brown ink, with brown and grey wash.

17¾ x 30in. (455 x 763mm).

This shows the whole length of the bridge, with its buildings, seen from King's Staith.

York City Art Gallery R1804.

YAT Collection VI 1 1.

Almost identical version in Birmingham City Museums and Art Gallery, pen and brown ink with grey wash on cream (1953 P174).

It contains much useful detail, from the figures on the staith to the suggestion of dilapidation on the bridge. The King's Arms, on the right, is shown with timber framing and exposed rubble walls; later views show plaster rendering.

68. *1784   The Old Ouse Bridge, York*

Joseph Farington. Oil on canvas.

From the same viewpoint as no.67, but with rather less detail and a less accurate view through the westernmost arch.

York, Merchant Adventurers' Hall.

69. *1791   Ouse Bridge at York from an Arch under the Town-Hall, 13th June 1791*

John White Abbot. Watercolour.

View from Common Hall Lane showing the north side of the bridge and part of the west bank of the river.

York City Art Gallery R2695.

See also: *The Ouse Bridge, York*

John White Abbot. Aquatint.

Similar to R2695, but not an exact copy.

York City Art Gallery R2647.

70. *c.1796   Ouse Bridge and St William's Chapel from downstream*

Thomas Girtin. Watercolour.

York City Art Gallery R1704.

Fig.65 (no.67) *This view by Farington is valuable because it portrays the full extent of the bridge. It shows timber supports under the private buildings on the right. The line of rough masonry and grass on the bridge façade is probably where houses and buildings were once supported. Some of the corbels shown here have now been incorporated into the wall on the King's Staith (see Fig.44, p.61). The river wall and Lendal Tower can be seen through the central arch of the bridge. This picture makes clear how important the Ouse was for trade; a barrel is being drawn up on to the staith and other cargo is ready for loading.*

71. *c.1796 Old Ouse Bridge, York*

Thomas Girtin. Watercolour.

View from the north, showing four arches of the bridge, the chapel and council chamber. It is valuable because it shows more of the council chamber than most pictures.

British Museum, LB43.

Evelyn Collection 93 (YAYAS, Minster Library).

72. 1797 *York, Ouse Bridge and Minster from downstream, midriver, 1797* (Fig.66)

J.M.W. Turner. Pencil sketch.

View from the south.

Tate Gallery, 'Tweed and Lakes' sketchbook, TB xxxv 69.

Reproduced in Hill 1996, pl.210.

Today, only the King's Arms is visible in this form from this viewpoint. The chapel, bridge and other buildings have gone; the tower of St Michael Spurriergate (at right) has been lowered; the Minster never was visible from this point, and must have been sketched later, from the bridge. It is, nevertheless, an attractive and lively composition. Turner does not appear to have produced a finished watercolour, either because such

a 'picturesque' scene was becoming less popular with artists, or because it had gone by the time he was producing illustrations for *Picturesque Views in England and Wales* 30 years later.

73. 1800 *Ouse Bridge, York* (Fig.67)

Thomas Girtin. Watercolour and pen and brown ink over pencil, with scratching out, on laid paper.

13 x 20½in. (329 x 524mm).

View from the east bank, showing the bridge from the south, with the chapel and other buildings at the south-west end, together with the King's Staith.

Yale Center for British Art (Paul Mellon Collection) B1977.14.363.

Evelyn Collection 142 (YAYAS, Minster Library).

Colour reproduction in Hill 1999, 51, pl.32.

Black and white reproduction in Morris 1986, 71, pl.77.

See also: ***1824 Old Ouse Bridge, York, 7 May 1824***

W. Reynolds, after Girtin. Mezzotint.

York City Art Gallery R1767, R4513 and R4517.

74. *n.d. (c.1800) Ouse Bridge and St William's Chapel*

John Claude Nattes. Pen and ink drawing.

View from the north.

York City Art Gallery R2933.

75. *n.d. (c.1800) Ouse Bridge and St William's Chapel* (dated, but indecipherable)

John Claude Nattes. Pen and ink drawing.

View from the east bank of the river, north of the bridge.

York City Art Gallery R2934.

The perspective is unhappy. Probably most useful for the view of the west bank of the river, seen through the central arch of the bridge.

76. *n.d. Ouse Bridge and St William's Chapel* (Fig.68)

Thomas Taylor. Watercolour.

View from the north-east, with the east and north elevations of the chapel.

York City Art Gallery R1442.

Fig.66   (no.72) Turner came to York in 1797, the year after his friend Girtin. He stayed in the same places and chose the same subjects to draw. Turner's depiction of the central arch from mid-stream in this pencil sketch is probably more accurate than Girtin's more flattened arch viewed from the King's Staith (see Fig.67).

Fig.67   (no.73) Girtin's watercolour of the bridge and chapel, looking downstream, c.1800. The chapel is shown clearly because the buildings on the other side of the road have been demolished. There are some inaccuracies in the background which seems very elevated on the right. This may be because Girtin was in York in 1796 but did not finish the picture until four years later.

[Ouse Bridge, York, 1800 (watercolour, pen and brown ink over pencil on paper) by Thomas Girtin (1775–1802). Yale Center for British Art, Paul Mellon Collection, USA. Photo: Bridgeman Art Library.]

Fig.68 *(no.76) This undated watercolour, probably painted c.1808, makes clear how narrow (from north to south) the central arch of the bridge was by comparison with the width of the arches carrying buildings at the west end. It also presents a clear view of the north side of the chapel and council chamber. The boat in the foreground has its mast lowered and there seems to be smoke coming from a small chimney. There is a largish boat just passing under the bridge with sweeps (oars) to take it upstream and another large boat with sails on the far side of the bridge. There is some sort of protective fencing and supports on the left (east) side of the bridge.*

77. 1801   *Old Ouse Bridge and St William's Chapel*

From a drawing by Thomas Taylor. Etching, aquatint with hand colouring.

Published 1811 by T. Taylor, Commercial Street, Leeds.

View from the north-east.

York City Art Gallery R4149.

Also in the Art Gallery:

Copy (faded), inscribed 'presented to the Merchants' Company'.

Also etching and aquatint, hand coloured, 'from an original drawing by T. Taylor, taken in 1806 and exhibited at the Royal Academy in 1808'.

Reproduced in Buttery 1984, 17.

A lively scene showing sailing barges with masts unstepped, and figures on the river bank (possibly washerwomen).

78. 1802   *Ouse Bridge from the South-East* (Fig.42, p.60)

Thomas White. Pen, ink and watercolour.

View from the King's Staith.

York City Art Gallery R1701.

Evelyn Collection 187 (YAYAS, Minster Library).

YAT Collection VI 1 2 (two copies).

79. 1803   *Part of Ouse Bridge, York, August 1803* (Fig.21, p.33)

Unknown artist. Pencil drawing.

View through the easternmost arch towards the King's Staith.

York City Art Gallery R2406

A clear and detailed view of the arch and the pillar supporting buildings on the bridge.

Cf. Figs.50 and 65.

80. *n.d.   Ouse Bridge*

Henry Cave. Pencil and wash.

York City Art Gallery R115.

81. *n.d.   Ouse Bridge, York*

Henry Cave. Large wash drawing.

View from the south-west.

York City Art Gallery W172.

In poor condition, but an interesting, wide-angle view showing a good deal of activity on the Queen's Staith.

82. *The Old Ouse Bridge and King's Staith*

Edwin Ridsdale Tate after Henry Cave. Sketch.

View from the south-west.

Old York Views 1905, 35.

This view from the Queen's Staith shows the south side of the bridge and King's Staith with buildings behind. The buildings over the second arch from the west have been recently removed. A good view both in general and in detail.

83. *1803   Ouse Bridge York*

John Sell Cotman. Three sketches.

a)   Pencil sketch.

5 x 9in. (127 x 230mm).

Inscribed on the back with notes on colour and 'July 4th 1803/Ouse Bridge, York'.

View from downstram, west bank of the river.

Norwich Castle Museum.

Reproduced in Rajnai and Allthorpe-Guyton 1979, pl.12.

b)   Pencil.

4¾ x 9¼in. (120 x 235mm).

Inscribed 'No.2 Ouse Bridge/July 5th 1803'.

View as above, but from further downstream.

Victoria and Albert Museum E724-1925.

c)   Pencil and brown wash.

7½ x 14½in. (190 x 368mm).

Signed and dated 'J.S. Cotman/1803'.

View downstream from the east bank.

Victoria and Albert Museum E3795-1934.

Reproduced in Kitson 1937, fig.12.

84. *1803   Children Swimming under the Ouse Bridge, York* (Fig.20, p.32)

John Varley. Watercolour.

15 x 21¼in. (380 x 540mm).

Close-up view of the second arch from the west, north side.

York City Art Gallery R3644.

A valuable view, showing the ribs of the arch, the starlings and the timber support of the bridge. The small window may relate to the former kidcote.

85. *c.1805   Old Ouse Bridge*

Attributed to John Varley. Pencil, watercolour and bodycolour with scratching out.

Previously attributed to David Cox.

14¾ x 19¼in. (377 x 493mm).

View from the south-east, with Albion Wharf in the foreground at left.

York City Art Gallery R1703.

Colour reproduction in Murray et al. 1990, pl.67.

Shows the bridge in context, though not all the buildings are accurately depicted.

86. *n.d. Old Ouse Bridge* (Fig.69)

After John Varley. Watercolour.

View from the south-west, showing the full width of the bridge.

York City Art Gallery R124.

87. *c.1807   Ouse Bridge, York*

John Varley. Grey and brown wash on rough brown paper.

4¼ x 10in. (110 x 255mm).

View from the south-east.

Eton College Gallery Pi 193 (306), from the Pilkington Collection.

This painting was done on the spot at twilight, showing the effect of light and weather on the buildings.

88. *(published) 1805   The Old Ouse Bridge, York* (Fig.70)

Edward Dayes. Engraving (W. and G. Cooke).

Published in Dayes 1825, 189.

Published in Brayley n.d., 179.

The *Picturesque Tour* appears in several editions, with slight variations in the title.

Single copies:

York City Art Gallery R4509. Dated 1805.

R4516. Proof copy, ripped.

R4522. Print published by Mrs Dayes.

Minster Library YK226 and YK227.

89. *1805   The Ouse Bridge, York*

Bartholomew Howlett. Engraving.

Published in Bigland 1805.

Minster Library YK224 and YK225.

Also: *1805 The Ouse Bridge, York*

John Roffe. Engraving.

Published in Bigland 1805.

York City Art Gallery (after Howlett) R4515.

Minster Library YK232.

City of Wakefield Museum, Gott Collection, 1805/6/80.

Fig.69 *(no.86) This view from the south-west shows the west bank of the river, now Queen's Staith. It shows clearly how the westernmost arch of the bridge had been extended southwards to support two shops. The two western arches had also been built out to the north, probably in the medieval period, for the chapel (see Fig.78, facing p.102). There seems to be timber fencing over the arch to the west of the central arch, probably erected as a safety measure after the removal of part of the debtors' prison. There are iron railings on the central arch and the arch to its east which had not been extended outwards. The Minster is shown with a turret on its tower, dating this painting to before 1808. The tower of St Michael Spurriergate on the right cannot be seen from the same viewpoint today because its tower was reduced in height in 1966.*

90. **1807   *Ouse Bridge and St William's Chapel*** (Fig.39, p.58)

Joseph Halfpenny. Etching.

9 x 11¼in. (230 x 285mm).

View from the north.

Halfpenny 1807, pl.21.

Single copies in York City Art Gallery R2370 and R3521.

Evelyn Collection 13 (YAYAS, Minster Library).

See p.57 for Halfpenny's comments on the measurements and shape of the arch.

91. **n.d. (c.1800–8)   *Part of Old Ouse Bridge*** (Fig.49, p.66)

Henry Cave. Wash drawing (preliminary sketch).

From the east bank of the river, north of the bridge.

York City Art Gallery R3085.

The east end of the bridge, with the shore and buildings above on the left.

92. **1808   *North view, Old Ouse Bridge and St William's Chapel***

Artist unknown: 'after an Original Drawing at the Royal Academy'.

View from the south.

York City Art Gallery R4532 and R4532.1.

93. **n.d.   *Old Ouse Bridge and St William's Chapel, frosty morning at 6 o'clock***

Henry Cave. Watercolour.

Atmospheric view from the west bank looking downstream.

York City Art Gallery R3047.

Fig.70 *(no.88) There was fierce debate between artists over the shape of the central arch of Ouse Bridge. It is in fact a catenarian arch (see pp.57–8). Edward Dayes was very critical of artists who showed the central arch of Ouse Bridge as pointed, commenting 'It is a singular circumstance, that most of the persons who have drawn this Bridge, have described the centre arch as a pointed one; perhaps this error may have arisen from the immensity of the arch, as the intersection of the opposite side, to the spectator, presents an angle so exceedingly sharp, as to deceive a superficial observer into a belief of its being really pointed' (Dayes 1805, 191). This view shows the river being used for trade, with what may well be coal being unloaded from a barge which has moored on the west bank. It also shows the Minster with the turret on its tower.*

94. 1809   View of Ouse Bridge, York, with St William's Chapel, as it stood in August 1809

Engraved by J. Le Keux from a drawing by Henry Cave for Hargrove's *History of York.*

Engraved on india paper 'from an original painting owned by R. Stephenson of York'.

View from King's Staith.

York City Art Gallery R4512.

Print in Hargrove 1818, 256.

95. n.d. (c.1809)   Ouse Bridge and St William's Chapel (Fig.46, p.63)

Unknown artist. Gouache.

View from the east bank of the river along the north side of the bridge towards the east end of the chapel.

York City Art Gallery R747.

96. n.d. (c.1809)   Old Ouse Bridge (Fig.71)

Henry Cave/Hilton. Oil on canvas.

Mansion House, York.

97. 1811   Ouse Bridge

Revd Charles H. Annesley. Chalk.

View from the south, including St William's Chapel. Industrial scene behind.

York City Art Gallery R325.

98. 1812   Ouse Bridge 1807 [sic]

Henry Cave. Pencil and watercolour.

View from King's Staith towards the west end of the bridge, with the east end and its buildings on the right.

York City Art Gallery R3044.

99. *n.d.   Ouse Bridge*

George Shepherd. Pencil and watercolour.

View from the west end of the bridge, indicating the steep incline of the roadway over the central arch.

York City Art Gallery R429.

100. *1816   Ouse Bridge, York*

John Varley. Engraving.

Minster Library YK241.

101. *1816   Ouse Bridge and part of King's Staith, Oct. 6 1816* (Fig.50, p.66)

Henry Cave. Pencil and watercolour.

The south side of the bridge from the King's Staith.

York City Art Gallery R13.

Evelyn Collection 39 (YAYAS, Minster Library).

See also Evelyn Collection 23.

102. *n.d.   Ouse Bridge, York*

F. Atkinson. Engraving.

Minster Library YK247.

103. *n.d.   Old Ouse Bridge, from a sketch by Girtin*

W.J. Barrett. Watercolour.

York City Art Gallery R131.

104. *1819   The Ouse Bridge, York, July 1819*

A member of the Lines family of Birmingham. Pencil sketch.

220 x 447mm.

View of the eastern half of the old bridge from King's Staith, showing the present King's Arms and neighbouring double-gabled building. The bridge had in fact been demolished for some years by 1819. The Lines were a family of artists working in Birmingham in the early 19th century. They all had a similar

Fig.71   (no.96) Ouse Bridge from Queen's Staith, with the city and Minster in the background. It presents a clear and detailed depiction of the full width of the bridge with much activity on both the river and the shore. This painting was presented to the city corporation by Lord Dundas on 4th February 1822.

artistic style so it is not always possible to identify individual members of the family.

City of Birmingham Museums and Art Gallery 1977 V80.

105. *1828   The Ouse-Bridge, York*

Etched by John Charles Varrall from a sketch by the late John Carter, F.S.A., for Britton 1828.

Inscribed 'To Peter Atkinson Esqr. Architect, of York, this Plate is inscribed by the Author'.

5 x 8¾in. (125 x 200mm).

View from the north-east.

Minster Library YK237.

Also, as above, hand coloured (Fig.24, p.38).

Private collection.

Carter's sketch was probably made in 1806.

106. *1835   Ouse Bridge*

George Pyne. Watercolour.

A clear and attractive view, though probably a copy.

York City Art Gallery R397.

107. *1836   Ouse Old Bridge, City Gaol and St William's Chapel*

Henry Brown. Wood engraving.

View from downstream, near King's Staith.

Brown and Brown 1836.

A copy, lively rather than accurate.

Also, as above, wood engraving on waxed paper.

York City Art Gallery R4511.

108. *n.d.   Ouse Bridge, York*

Ann James Bowman. Watercolour.

View from downstream, east bank of the river.

York City Art Gallery R4.

Interesting use of colour; little detail and not entirely accurate.

109. *n.d.   Ouse Bridge and St William's Chapel*

Artist unknown, 'after Taylor'. Ink and watercolour.

View from the north.

York City Art Gallery R115.

Clear detail of the stonework.

110. *c.1907   Old Ouse Bridge, York, in 1807*

Edwin Ridsdale Tate. Colour print.

Published as a greetings card by Arthur and Co., Stonegate.

Copied from Halfpenny 1807, pl.21 (see Fig.39, p.58).

North Yorkshire Library Service.

Buildings on Ouse Bridge

111. *1736   Ouse-bridge at York* (Fig.40, p.59)

William Henry Toms. Engraving.

7½ x 12in. (190 x 310mm).

View from the south.

Drake 1736, opposite p.281.

Evelyn Collection 24 (YAYAS, Minster Library).

A stylised view of the bridge, with some details shown clearly. The naval vessels and other boats shown are somewhat fanciful and probably never actually sailed on the Ouse.

112. *1782   Plan of Ouse Bridge* (Fig.22, p.34)

Dr William White. Ink drawing.

YAT Collection MP26.

Evelyn Collection 8 (YAYAS, Minster Library).

This plan/south elevation of the bridge shows shops, the gaol and Ouse Bridge Hall (the council chamber and chapel combined by that date).

113. *1960   Stained glass depicting the medieval bridge (Fig.45, p.62)*

H.W. Harvey. Detail from the Guildhall west window.

St William's Chapel

114. *1810   St William's Chapel, Ouse Bridge* (Fig.25, p.39)
Ground plan. Date given overleaf as 1800.
Evelyn Collection 51 (YAYAS, Minster Library).
YAT Collection VI 2 8.

115. *n.d.   Ousegate*
Francis Place. Pencil and wash.
View of part of Ouse Bridge from the north, with St William's Chapel.
York City Art Gallery R1956b.

116. *1749   Pillars and Arches in the entient Chapel of St William on Ouse-Bridge, York*
Measured drawing, scale given.
From *Drawings of Saxon Churches* (Society of Antiquaries, F12).
RCHM negative YSW 320.
YAT Collection VI 2 5.

117. *1749   The Porch of Ousebridge Chapel, York*
Measured drawing, scale given.
From *Drawings of Saxon Churches* (Society of Antiquaries, F14).
RCHM negative YSW 321.
YAT Collection VI 2 3.
Shows the porch and door with the window above.

118. *1749   The Porch to the Chapel on Ouse Bridge, York*
Measured drawing, scale given.
From *Drawings of Saxon Churches* (Society of Antiquaries, F17).
RCHM negative YSW 322.
YAT Collection VI 2 4.
A more detailed view of the porch. Includes a note that the cherubim's head and the coats of arms are modern additions. Architectural fragments from the porch are now in the Yorkshire Museum (see Fig.32, p.45).
See also Evelyn Collection 138–41 (YAYAS, Minster Library).

119. *1776   North East Prospect of the Hall upon Ouse Bridge*
Edward Abbot? Wash drawing.
A fairly standard view of the chapel and part of the bridge.
Wakefield Art Gallery, Gott Collection 1776/3/11.

120. *1790   Ouse Bridge and St William's Chapel*
After Place. Engraving.
York City Art Gallery R4535.

121. *1797   York, Ouse Bridge and St William's Chapel*
J.M.W. Turner. Pencil sketch.
10¾ x 14½in. (274 x 370mm).
View from the north-east, showing the north side of the bridge and the east and north sides of the chapel.
Tate Gallery, 'Tweed and Lakes' sketchbook, TB xxxv, 72.
Reproduced in Hill 1996, 144, pl.209.

122. *1803–5   The Old Ouse Bridge and St William's Chapel*
John Varley. Pencil and watercolour.
9¼ x 13¾in. (232 x 347mm).
A similar view to no.121, with clear depiction of many details.
York City Art Gallery R249.

123. *n.d. (c.1803)   St William's Chapel, Ouse Bridge*
Attributed to John Varley, but possibly by a pupil. Watercolour.
View from the east bank of the river, showing the east and part of the north sides of the chapel, with part of the bridge.
York City Art Gallery R263.

124. *n.d. (c.1803)   St William's Chapel and Bridge*
John Varley. Watercolour.
View from the west bank of the river, upstream. A general outline, with little detail, but much human and canine activity in the river.
York City Art Gallery R380.

125. *1805   St William's Chapel and Ouse Bridge, looking downstream, 1805*
Henry Cave. Watercolour.
View from the east bank of the river, looking towards the chapel.
York City Art Gallery R3046.

126. *1807   Ouse Bridge and St William's Chapel* (Fig.72)
Joseph Halfpenny. Etching.
9 x 11¼in. (230 x 285mm).
A very clear view of the north side of the bridge and the east end of the chapel.
Halfpenny 1807, pl.22.
Single print in York City Art Gallery R2371.
Evelyn Collection 12 (YAYAS, Minster Library).

127. *1807   Entrance to St William's Chapel* (Fig.26, p.40)
Joseph Halfpenny. Etching.
11¼ x 9in. (285 x 230mm).

Fig.72 *(no.126) This view of the east end of the chapel shows its relationship with the bridge, built over an extended arch. The east end was rebuilt in the 13th century (probably in 1268), with a fine three-light window and small side lancets, the latter blocked up by this time. The picture shows the chapel's unusual roofline, with a more steeply pitched roof over the central aisle than over the two side aisles. The tiny windows below the chapel belonged to the kidcote (prison). The chapel has a wooden louvred turret and spire, topped by a weather vane. There are decorative corbels just below the roof on the north elevation but the three decorative finials at the east end may be later additions. The wooden prop on the right is shown in several pictures.*

Halfpenny 1807, pl.23.

Halfpenny omits the cherub's head shown in other drawings (see no.118 and Fig.27, p.40).

128. *1807   Ornaments in St William's Chapel* (Fig.73)

Joseph Halfpenny. Etching.

9¾ x 7¾in. (245 x 187mm).

Halfpenny 1807, frontispiece.

Single print in York City Art Gallery R2350.

Evelyn Collection 47 (YAYAS, Minster Library).

Part of the late 12th-century screen and other fragments of carved masonry.

129. *n.d. (c.1809)   Ouse Bridge and St William's Chapel*

George Nicholson. Pencil drawing.

The north side, seen from east bank of the river.

York City Art Gallery R1381.

130. *n.d. (c.1809)   Ouse Bridge and St William's Chapel*

George Nicholson. Pencil drawing.

View from the south.

York City Art Gallery R906.

131. *n.d. (c.1809)   Part of Old Ouse Bridge and St William's Chapel, sketched during its demolition*

George Nicholson. Pencil sketch.

View of the north side from the west bank, showing arches, windows, three gables and belfry.

York City Art Gallery, Nicholson Sketchbooks R2446 (90).

Fig.73 *(no.128) A stylised view of the screen and dismantled masonry from the screen. There is a clear depiction of the three carved heads (see also Fig.28, p.41), but the representation of the height of the arches is not accurate.*

FRAGMENTA VETUSTA OR THE REMAINS OF ANCIENT BUILDINGS IN YORK. drawn and etched by JOSEPH HALFPENNY. MDCCCVII.

132. *n.d. (c.1809)* *York, St William's Chapel, Ouse Bridge, East end*

George Nicholson. Watercolour.

The east elevation of the chapel, from across the river.

'Sketches from Nature in Various Parts of the Kingdom', no.11.

York City Art Gallery, Nicholson Sketchbooks, R5135 (10).

YAT Collection VI 2 2.

133. *n.d. (c.1809)* *St William's Chapel, Ouse Bridge, North side*

George Nicholson. Pencil and wash drawing.

York City Art Gallery R697.

A good view of the north and east sides of the chapel, the north side of the council chamber and the houses beyond.

134. *n.d.* *Ouse Bridge and St William's Chapel*

Henry Cave. Watercolour.

Shows the north side of the chapel only.

York City Art Gallery R3045.

135. *n.d.* *Part of Old Ouse Bridge and St William's Chapel*

Henry Cave. Pencil sketch.

Sketch from immediately below the chapel on the north side, showing the windows, bell tower and the buttresses beneath the bridge.

York City Art Gallery R3048.

136. *n.d.   Ouse Bridge and St William's Chapel*

Henry Cave. Wash drawing.

From the east bank of the river, north of the bridge.

York City Art Gallery, R3045.

137. *n.d.   St William's Chapel and Old Ouse Bridge*

Henry Cave. Colour wash over pencil.

From the west bank, north of the bridge, with no great detail.

York City Art Gallery R3046.

138. *c.1810   Sketch of interior looking East during demolition*

Henry Cave. Pencil sketch.

10 x 13¾in. (254 x 352mm).

York City Art Gallery R3050.

RCHM negative YSW 473.

YAT Collection VI 2 7.

Evelyn Collection 41 and 45 (YAYAS, Minster Library).

Reproduced in RCHMY **3**, pl.145.

The building is roofless. On the left, there are two bays on the north side, with blind arcading (the Easter Sepulchre) behind. In the centre are the three lancets of the east window and on the right a bay on the south side lightly sketched in.

139. *1813 (published)   The Inside of St William's Chapel* (Fig.30, p.43)

Henry Cave. Engraving.

7¾ x 9¾in. (200 x 250mm).

As no.138, but a slightly closer view, with details filled in. Cave notes that his interior views were drawn 'while the chapel was in a state of actual dilapidation'.

Cave 1813, pl.XXIV.

Single print in York City Art Gallery R2280.

Original drawing in York City Art Gallery R3478.

Evelyn Collection 54 (YAYAS, Minster Library).

Also: As above, with glass in the window and an extra pillar on the left.

H. Cave. Pencil.

York City Art Gallery R3050.

140. *c.1810   Interior during demolition* (Fig.48, p.65)

Henry Cave. Pencil sketch.

9¾ x 13¾in. (250 x 352mm).

View looking west.

York City Art Gallery R3049.

RCHM negative YSW 474.

YAT Collection VI 2 6.

Reproduced in Murray et al. 1990, pl.61 and in RCHMY **3**, pl.145.

Workmen are demolishing the west end. The screen remains, together with the westernmost arcades and the blind arcading on the north wall. The north wall of the council chamber is still standing, with a window, but the rest has gone, revealing a timber-framed building behind.

141. *1813 (published)   The Screen of St William's Chapel* (Fig.29, p.42)

Henry Cave. Engraving.

7¾ x 9¾in. (198 x 246mm).

Cave 1813, pl.XXVII.

Single print in York City Art Gallery R2287.

Original drawing, dated 12 August 1809, in York City Art Gallery R3475.

See also Evelyn Collection 42–4 and 49 (YAYAS, Minster Library).

142. *c.1810   Ouse Bridge*

Henry Cave. Pencil sketch.

Previously attributed to J. Harper.

York City Art Gallery R1693.

Drawn from the west bank of the river, on the south side and almost immediately below St William's Chapel. It shows the arch and pier of the bridge, and the south doorway and window of the chapel still standing, though scaffolding has been erected and workmen are removing the roof.

143. *1807 (1817?)   King's Staithe*

Henry Cave. Wash drawing.

View from the west bank, below the chapel on the north side.

York City Art Gallery R3044.

144. *n.d.   Part of Old Ouse Bridge and St William's Chapel*

Henry Cave. Pencil sketch.

Detail of the north side of the chapel and the triple gable of the council chamber.

York City Art Gallery R3048.

145. *1809/1820   Old Ouse Bridge and St William's Chapel, from sketches made previous to the demolition of the chapel in August 1809*

Henry Cave. Etching.

York City Art Gallery R4512.

Minster Library YK223.

Reproduced in VCHY, frontispiece.

146. *1813   The Entrance into St William's Chapel* (Fig.27, p.40)

Henry Cave. Engraving.

Cave 1813, pl.XXV.

Single print in York City Art Gallery R2283.

Original drawing in York City Art Gallery R3477.

See also Evelyn Collection 32–4 (YAYAS, Minster Library).

cf. Nos.117–18.

147. 1813 *St William's Chapel and part of Micklegate* (Fig.41, p.59)

Henry Cave. Engraving.

7¾ x 9¾in. (198 x 257mm).

View from the east end of Ouse Bridge, showing the east and south elevations of the chapel. The illustration also indicates the steep rise of the roadway over the central arch of the bridge.

Cave 1813, pl.XXIII.

Single print in York City Art Gallery R2278.

Original drawing in York City Art Gallery R3479.

Evelyn Collection 17 and 21 (YAYAS, Minster Library).

148. 1813 *Part of the Screen in St William's Chapel* (Fig.28, p.41)

Henry Cave. Engraving.

9¾ x 7¾in. (247 x 196mm).

Detail of the 12th-century carving on the screen, drawn during demolition.

Cave 1813, pl.XXVI.

Single print in York City Art Gallery R2285.

Original drawing in York City Art Gallery R3476.

See also Evelyn Collection 46 (south-west aisle) and 54 (YAYAS, Minster Library).

cf. Fig.73, p.95.

149. 1811 (published) *Ouse Bridge, York*

Edward Dayes, engraved by Hawkesworth. Published 30 June 1811 by Wm. Clark, new Bond Street.

View from the north side.

York City Art Gallery, R4520 and R4520.1.

Minster Library YK244.

150. 1817 *St William's Chapel, York*

John Greig. Engraving.

From the *Antiquarian Itinerary* 10th October 1817.

Minster Library YK248.

151. 1823 *Ouse Bridge and St William's Chapel*

J.C. Burgess. Pencil sketch.

A detailed and attractive sketch, but probably a copy. Similar to Fig.72, p.94.

York City Art Gallery R2698.

152. 1825 *Detailed sketch, with notes, of a carved stone from the Chapel*

Revd J. Skinner. Pencil drawing.

British Museum Add. MS 33684, fos.30v, 33.

The stone is a 13th-century reworking of part of a 12th-century arch. Revd J. Skinner identifies the low-relief carvings as representing the Annunciation and the Flight into Egypt. The carved stone is now in the Yorkshire Museum (HB 440; Fig.31, p.44).

See RCHMY 3, 50a and pl.141.

153. 1863 *Part of the Screen of St William's Chapel*

H.S. Smith. Lithograph.

Probably a copy of Cave 1813, pl.XXVI (Fig.28, p.41).

York City Art Gallery R903.

154. c.1907 *St William's Chapel and Briggate, York, in 1807*

Edwin Ridsdale Tate. Colour print from watercolour.

Card in possession of York Public Library.

View from the east end of Ouse Bridge, showing the east and south elevations of the chapel. Part of Briggate (now Bridge Street) and Micklegate beyond. Almost certainly copied from Cave 1813, pl.XXIII (Fig.41, p.59). There is a tracing of this by Ridsdale Tate in 'Old York Sketches . . . collected by George Benson' (York Public Library). This and Old Ouse Bridge, 1807 (no.110), were produced as postcards/greetings cards for Arthur and Co., printers of cards and sheet music, Stonegate (P. Stanhope, pers. comm.).

155. 1911 *North-West Corner of the Nave, St William's Chapel on Ouse Bridge, York* (Fig.74)

Edwin Ridsdale Tate. Pencil drawing.

York City Art Gallery R5443.

Evelyn Collection 49 (YAYAS, Minster Library).

A hypothetical reconstruction of part of the interior, probably based on the works of Halfpenny and Cave.

156. 1916 *Interior of St William's Chapel on Ouse Bridge, looking East* (Fig.75)

Edwin Ridsdale Tate. Pen and wash drawing.

York City Art Gallery R195.

Evelyn Collection 1283 (YAYAS, Minster Library).

Also (newspaper cutting) in 'Old York Sketches, Tracings etc., chiefly by Edwin Ridsdale Tate, collected by George Benson', p.113 (York Public Library).

This is a hypothetical reconstruction.

157. 1967 *Reconstruction of part of the screen at the west end of the chapel* (Fig.33, p.45)

Yorkshire Museum HB 434. Photograph.

RCHM negative YSW 1078.

See also Evelyn Collection 52–3 (YAYAS, Minster Library).

158. 1969 *End stone from the string course above the screen at the west end of the chapel* (Fig.34, p.46)

Yorkshire Museum HB 435–8. Photograph.

RCHM negative YC 1389.

Fig.74 (left; no155) This conjectural reconstruction by Ridsdale Tate shows the screen on the west wall of the chapel, with a small window at its north end. There is just the hint of the doorway into the council chamber, behind the column in the foreground. Ridsdale Tate's reconstruction of the timber roof of the central aisle and the lower roof of the north aisle is interesting (see exterior view of the roofline, Fig.72, p.94).

Fig.75 (below; no.156) Another conjectural reconstruction of the interior of the chapel. Ridsdale Tate has assumed a tiled floor and a raised tiled platform at the east end (both similar to those known to have existed in Bedern Chapel, AY 10/5, 549–50, figs.311–12). The main doorway in the south wall is open, with steps up to it, and the railing of the bridge is visible outside. The small window can be seen above the doorway and also the small window to the east of the door, which was not shown on the plan of 1810 (Fig.25, p.39). There is just the hint of a door in the north wall near the east end, though it is hard to know where this would lead to. The rafters again give a good idea of the shape of the roof. Ridsdale Tate has put together all that can be gleaned about the internal appearance of the chapel from other drawings produced before or during demolition.

159. *1967   Norman cable-mould voussoirs from the south doorway of St William's Chapel* (Fig.32, p.45)

Yorkshire Musuem HB 482. Photograph.

RCHM negative YSW 1079.

160. *1965   Carved voussoir from St William's Chapel* (Fig.31, p.44)

Yorkshire Museum HB 440. Photograph.

RCHM negative BB007797. © Crown copyright, NMR.

The Council Chamber

161. *1776   Old Common Hall and St William's Chapel from the South* (Fig.35, p.49)

Edward Abbot. Wash drawing.

Wakefield Art Gallery, Gott Collection 1776/3/12.

Evelyn Collection 1328 (YAYAS, Minster Library)

YAT Collection VI 2 1.

A rare unhindered view of the chapel and the council chamber from the south. The small door to the east of the main chapel door is not shown on the plan of 1810 (Fig.25, p.39). It may have led to a staircase to the lower level (see RCHMY **3**, 49).

162. *1905   York from Briggate 100 years ago* (Fig.36, p.50)

Edwin Ridsdale Tate. Drawing.

Conjectural reconstruction of the council chamber and chapel, as from the roof of a building on the south-west.

'Old York Sketches, Tracings etc., chiefly by Edwin Ridsdale Tate, collected by George Benson', p.96 (York Public Library).

Evelyn Collection 27 (YAYAS, Minster Library).

Reproduced on the cover of Old York Views, 1905.

See also:

Panorama from the West End of Ouse Bridge, York

Edwin Ridsdale Tate.

Evelyn Collection 2167 (YAYAS, Minster Library).

Ouse Bridge, 1810 onwards

163. *c.1810 Plans and elevations of the proposed new bridge* (Fig.51, p.67)

Peter Atkinson jr. Architect's measured drawings.

Folder labelled Ouse Bridge Drawings (Atkinson) in Borthwick Institute of Historical Research, University of York.

Twenty-seven (including one found in the archives of the Merchant Adventurers and given to the Borthwick Institute in 1990) plans and elevations of the proposed new bridge and adjoining streets, including preliminary plans as well as the one finally accepted, and detailed drawings showing construction methods and materials. The folder also includes one elevation of the proposed new Foss Bridge, dated 1811.

164. *c.1820 Peter Atkinson* (Figs.54–5, p.69)

Martin Archer Shee. Oil on canvas.

Portrait of the architect Peter Atkinson.

York City Art Gallery 1002.

165. *n.d. A Section through Ouse Bridge showing the Houses* (Fig.76)

Artist unknown. Competition Drawing no.8.

166. *n.d. Workmen pulling down the Houses for the Bridge Improvement* (Fig.47, p.64)

E. Ridsdale Tate. Tracing from H. Cave (c.1809).

'Old York Sketches, Tracings etc., chiefly by Edwin Ridsdale Tate, collected by George Benson', p.50 (York Public Library).

cf. Fig.78, facing p.102, and Cave 1813, pls.IV and XXXIII.

167. *1818 Ouse Bridge* (Fig.53, p.68)

J.M.W. Turner. Pencil sketch.

View from the north.

Tate Gallery, Turner Bequest, TB clix 65 as.

168. *1823 The Old Ouse Bridge, York, and The New Ouse Bridge, York* (Fig.56, p.70)

Henry Cave. Lithographs, printed by C. Hullmandel.

Each image 1¾ x 5¾in. (45 x 149mm).

Viewed from King's Staith.

York City Art Gallery R1763.

Evelyn Collection 25 (YAYAS, Minster Library).

Reproduced in Murray et al. 1990, pl.59.

Also, as above:

Pencil drawing, York City Art Gallery R2864.

Lithograph, York City Art Gallery R2862.

169. *c.1836 Ouse Bridge* (Fig.77)

C. Dillon. Watercolour.

View looking east across the bridge, showing industrial buildings, and the hustle and bustle of daily life.

Evelyn Collection 2032 (YAYAS, Minster Library).

170. *1919 Plan of Ouse Bridge c.1807 and Plan of the First Stone Bridge c.1240* (Fig.78)

George Benson. Measured plan.

Benson 1919, fig.43, facing p.88.

The plan of the 1240 bridge is partly conjectural. The plan of c.1807 is from a survey made by Peter Atkin-

Fig.76 *(no.165) The houses proposed c.1809 are similar to those which were actually built on the north-west side of Ousegate and which still stand today, differing only in proportion. This picture shows that changes in the approaches to the bridge, in both Bridge Street and Ousegate, were already under consideration. In this cross-section the piers right up to the roadway are of solid ashlar, but the spandrels and the abutments are filled with rubble (information from notes made by the late D.W. Black who, with E.A. Gee, studied all the plans and elevations of the proposed new bridge in 1965).*

Fig.77   *(no.169) Dillon's watercolour of c.1836 is valuable because it places Ouse Bridge in the context of 19th-century York.*

son for the new bridge and approaches, and is super-imposed in red on a plan of the 1565 bridge.

Some of the dates given by Benson need to be corrected (see below).

See also Evelyn Collection 3–6, plans by Barker (YAYAS, Minster Library).

171. *1943   Ouse Bridge*
Patrick Hall. Etching.
View from the south, including King's Staith.
York City Art Gallery R4514.

172. *1943   Ouse Bridge from Queen's Staith*
Joseph Southall. Pencil, watercolour and bodycolour.
14¾ x 20½in. (375 x 520mm).
York City Art Gallery R511.
Reproduced in Murray et al. 1990, pl.60.
View from the south-west, with the bridge and 19th-century buildings in Low Ousegate.

Fig.78   *(facing; no.170) Benson's plans are useful for a comparison between the medieval stone bridge (which he has dated c.1240, but which should probably be earlier, c.1170), the 1565 bridge and the proposed new bridge (in red). This illustration is also helpful in locating the chapel, the council chamber and the toll booth.*

Select Index of Maps of York showing the River Ouse and Ouse Bridge

c.1610 'Yorke' by John Speed[e]

Ouse Bridge is labelled (no.17) but there is no representation of St William's Chapel.

Theatre of the Empire of Great Britain by John Speed[e] (1610); map of the West Riding of Yorkshire, with inset plan of York.

York City Library: no.1 in map drawer.

YAT Collection MP2.

1694 'The Ichonography or Ground Plot of ye City of York survey'd by Benedict Horsley, 1694' (printed 1697)

Some attempt at accurate, as opposed to symbolic, representation of Ouse Bridge (no.29), with St William's Chapel. Also shows 'Ye 3 Water Lanes' (no.41). Arrows show the direction in which the river flowed.

British Museum Maps, K45, 1.

York City Library: no.6 in map drawer.

YAT Collection MP5.

c.1727 'A New and Exact Plan of the City of York' by John Cossins (1st edition)

Again, some attempt at realism. Ouse Bridge is shown with a large central arch and two smaller arches at each side, and with a steep slope up to the centre from each side. It shows St William's Chapel, with its spire, at the Micklegate end. The House of Correction is labelled (L). Three water lanes are labelled, as is the ferry next to the Water Tower at Lendal.

British Museum Maps, K45, 3.

York City Library: no.22 in map drawer.

YAT Collection MP6.

Reproduced in Murray 1997, 18–19.

1736 'A Plan of the City of York' by Francis Drake

Ouse Bridge is portrayed with its five arches and there is an attempt to show shops and houses on the bridge as well as the chapel with its spire. Ouse Bridge and the Town Hall are labelled (no.21). Ferries and water lanes are not labelled.

YAT Collection MP7.

Drake 1736, 244.

1750 'Map of York' by Peter Chassereau

Ouse Bridge is represented as though viewed from above, but five arches are still indicated, the central one being the widest. There is no representation of St William's Chapel. Two ferries are labelled, one next to North Street Postern

and the other next to Skeldergate Postern. 'The crane' at Skeldergate is labelled, as are the three water lanes between King's Staith and Nessgate. The New Walk is represented by a double row of trees.

York City Library: no.11 in map drawer.

YAT Collection MP8.

Reproduced in Murray et al. 1990, 70, pl.56.

1760 'A Plan of the City of York' by Ann Todd

Ouse Bridge is shown with a large central arch and two smaller arches at each side, but rather flattened in appearance. It shows St William's Chapel, with its spire. King's Staith is labelled and also 'crane house'. An arrow shows the direction in which the river flowed.

YAT Collection MP9.

1772 'Map of York, Published according to Act of Parliament 25 March 1772' by T. Jefferys

Ouse Bridge is shown viewed from above. St William's Chapel is not drawn or labelled but two buildings shown west of the bridge at the bottom of Micklegate are labelled 'Town Hall' and 'City Goal' (sic). Both ferries are labelled and also the three water lanes. The New Walk is represented by a double row of trees, but is labelled 'Long Walk'.

York City Library: no.12 in map drawer.

YAT Collection MP10.

See Fig.7, p.11.

1782 Plans by Dr William White, January 1782

The Ouse Bridge plan shows the steep angle up from each side to the centre, Ouse Bridge Hall with a weather vane and opposite Ouse Bridge Gaol. It also gives the names and trades of people with shops on the bridge.

York City Library: no.14 in map drawer.

YAT Collection MP26.

See Fig.22, p.34.

1785 'City and Ainsty' by Francis White

There is no attempt at a realistic representation of Ouse Bridge, and St William's Chapel is simply labelled (no.23). Other features labelled include North Street Postern and the Water Works, 1st, 2nd and 3rd Water Lane, 'Friers Walls', Skeldergat (sic) Postern and the nearby ferry, and New Walk. An arrow shows the direction in which the river flowed.

York City Library: no.23 in map drawer.

YAT Collection MP12.

Select Index of Artists and Photographers

Abbot, Edward, fl. 1774–6

Produced many coloured wash drawings of buildings in and around York in 1774–6, possibly intended to illustrate a new edition of Drake's *Eboracum* proposed by Thomas Beckwith. These are now in the Gott Collection, Wakefield City Art Gallery; black and white copies of some are in the Evelyn Collection of slides and in the YAT Collection. Some are signed by Abbot; others, similar in style and colouring but more assured, may be by him or by J. Beckwith. Though somewhat naïve, they are very valuable, representing a period otherwise barren in local topographical art; also many show aspects of buildings ignored by other artists.

Abbott, John White, 1763–1851

Surgeon and amateur artist, born in Exeter and lived in Devon, becoming Deputy-Lieutenant in 1831. Travelled north in 1791. Four watercolours of York are now in the City Art Gallery.

Atkinson, Peter, 1776–1843

Architect, son of Peter Atkinson who was the assistant and then partner of John Carr. Did work on the Female Debtors' prison in 1803. Won a competition for the design of the new Ouse Bridge, a three-arch bridge constructed in two stages. He was also responsible for the present Foss Bridge.

Bell, John, c.1827–81

Local landscape painter, highly regarded in York. Dismissed from the School of Design for being 'frolicsome'. Two of his river views of York are in the City Art Gallery.

Benson, George, 1856–1935

Architect and antiquary. His publication *York from its Origin to 1925* (3 volumes, 1911, 1919, 1925; reprinted 1968) includes his own plans and elevations of excavations and buildings, and he also published shorter articles. He produced a partly conjectural plan of the first stone bridge and a plan of Ouse Bridge as it was c.1807. His collection of 'Old York Sketches, Tracings etc., chiefly by Edwin Ridsdale Tate' in York Public Library contains many original drawings of considerable topographical interest. He was Curator of Archaeology and Numismatics at the Yorkshire Philosophical Society's Museum.

Boddy, William James, 1832–1911

Born in Woolwich; settled in York in 1853. Assistant to architects G. Fowler Jones and J.B. and W. Atkinson, then became full-time watercolour artist and teacher at several schools, including St Peter's in York and Ampleforth, until 1908. In 1905, 34 of his watercolours were reproduced in colour in *Historic York* (text by J.S. Fletcher) and local exhibitions of his work were held in 1911 and 1912. Most of his paintings are of well-known views, but some are from unusual angles or give detail not otherwise immediately available. Boddy exhibited at the Royal Academy and the Royal Society of British Artists between 1860 and 1890.

Boys, Thomas Shotter, 1803–74

Watercolour painter and lithographer, born in Pentonville. Exhibited at the Royal Academy 1824 and Paris 1827. Published views of Belgian and French cities and of London (this last in 1842). His ten lithographic views of York were published in 1841 and some watercolour scenes in the city also date from this period. Later, his career declined and he died in poverty. His work shows precise observation of architectural detail combined with scenes of cheerful, bustling human activity.

Britton, John, 1771–1857

Antiquary and topographer. Born near Chippenham, Wiltshire, and became a publisher of illustrated books in London, notably *The Beauties of England and Wales* (1801); *Architectural Antiquities of Great Britain* (1805–14); *Cathedral Antiquities* (1814–35); and, with Pugin, *Specimens of Gothic Architecture* (1823–5).

Brown, Henry, 1816–70, and William, 1814–77

Wood engravers, born in York. Published 83 engraved views of York in 1836 as well as several single engravings. Settled in the Netherlands from 1840, becoming successive Heads of the Royal School of Engraving at the Hague. Whilst their small drawings show a lack of concern for accuracy in measurement or perspective, they contain valuable details and the overall impression is often more perceptive than that of more precise draughtsmen.

Carter, John N., 1748–1817

Born in London. Fellow of the Society of Antiquaries 1795 and worked as its draughtsman. Travelled widely in England, visiting York in 1780 and 1806, and left 26 volumes of sketches. Publications include *Specimens of Antient Sculpture and Painting to Henry VIII* (1780–94); *Views of Ancient Buildings in England*, republished as *Specimens of Gothic Architecture* (enlarged edition by Britton, 1845); and a series of papers in the *Gentleman's Magazine*, 1798–1817. Here and elsewhere he was very critical of his contemporaries for their over-restoration or destruction of ancient buildings (for example, his letter about old Ouse Bridge quoted in Davies 1880, 202–4; see pp.65, 67). He has been described as '. . . irascible, quarrelsome, dogmatic, obstinate' but 'his integrity was incorruptible'.

Cave, Henry, 1779–1836

One of York's most important topographical artists. Son of William Cave, engraver. Born in York and lived in Micklegate. Art teacher in several York schools. He produced many drawings, etchings, watercolours and oils of scenes in and around York. In 1810 his *Picturesque Buildings in York* (also entitled *Antiquities of York*) was published, with 2nd and 3rd editions both dated 1813. York City Art Gallery has the etched copper plates and pencil drawings for this work, as well as prints. Cave exhibited work at the Royal Academy between 1814 and 1825. See Cooper 1911.

Cotman, John Sell, 1782–1842

Encouraged to draw when at school in Norwich. Moved to London, found employment with Ackermann and gained the patronage of Dr Munro. Through him got to known Girtin and became a member of the Sketching Club (founded by Girtin) and friend of Munn (q.v.). Between 1802 and 1804 Cotman helped Munn to produce drawings for young ladies to use for copying. These included the sketches made when touring together in Yorkshire in 1803. He was an artist ahead of his time in his use of bold colour, simple subject matter and composition, and his preoccupation with pattern and form.

Dayes, Edward, 1763–1804

Born in London, he first studied printmaking, then enrolled at the Royal Academy Schools in 1780 and began to exhibit at the Royal Academy in 1786. In the 1790s he was active in supplying drawings for topographical publications and working up sketches by amateur artists and antiquaries. Dayes' sketches have often been confused with early works by Turner and Girtin. The latter was a pupil of Dayes from 1788, but the two men quarrelled. According to popular (but unsubstantiated) legend, Dayes resented his pupil's success and had him imprisoned as a refractory apprentice. A meticulous draughtsman, he saw himself as an upholder of traditional standards in the face of the new and more dashing style. He committed suicide in 1804. See also Bibliography, p.112.

Drake, Nathan, 1727–78

Painter in oils and watercolour, a miniaturist and a drawing master. Probably born in Lincoln, but by 1752 he was living in York. On 29 January 1754 he was advertising the proposed publication by subscription of a print from his view of York from the New Walk Terrace, although in fact it was not ready until July 1756. Little is known of his later work. In 1771 he was elected a Fellow of the Society of Artists. He is buried in the church of St Michael-le-Belfrey.

Farington, Joseph, 1747–1821

Landscape painter and topographical draughtsman, born in Manchester. Went to London in 1763 and became one of the first pupils at the Royal Academy Schools. Undertook extensive sketching tours in the north of England and developed two main specialities, rivers and mountains. In 1781 he settled in London and became an influential figure in the Royal Academy. In his finished topographical drawings he first sketched the subject lightly in pencil, then added painstaking pen and black or brown ink outlines and finally a grey or brown wash, with occasional local colour such as blue. The whole effect is careful and self-controlled. See Clarke 1976.

Fenton, Roger (1819–69)

Born in Rochdale. Studied art and in Paris became interested in photography. Realised art could never support him so studied law, qulaifying as a solicitor in 1847 and called to the Bar in 1851. Appointed first secretary to the (Royal) Photographic Society in 1853 and by 1854 he was engaged totally in photography. Commissioned to take photographs of the royal family by Queen Victoria and was appointed photographer to the British Museum. In 1854 arrived in Yorkshire to try out a travelling dark room (necessary for the new collodion process) which he planned to take to the Crimea the following year to take pictures of the war. Took photographs of York Minster, but also of Lendal ferry and the River Ouse.

Gastineau, Henry, 1792–1876

Prolific 'picturesque' topographer in watercolour. Born in London of Huguenot origins and studied oil painting at the Royal Academy Schools. Became a member of the Old Watercolour Scoiety in 1823. Travelled widely in Britain, Switzerland and Italy, sometimes with his friend J.M.W. Turner, whose work influenced his style. From 1833 produced many drawings for topographical publications. He was a prolific artist and exhibited regularly for 58 years.

Girtin, Thomas, 1775–1802

Born in Southwark, London, and apprenticed to topographical watercolourist Edward Dayes (q.v.) in 1788. In 1794 he exhibited for the first time at the Royal Academy. Between 1795 and 1798 he went on summer sketching tours, making pencil sketches which were redrawn and coloured in the studio on his return to London. He first toured the north of England, including Yorkshire, in 1796, in search of the romantic and wild ruins of castles and abbeys. One of his chief patrons was Edward Lascelles, son of the 1st Earl of Harewood, and Girtin returned to the north regularly for the rest of his life. Between 1800 and 1801 he produced a series of watercolours of northern bridges: Harewood, Wetherby, Skellgate (near Ripon), Hawes and Morpeth, as well as Ouse Bridge in York. The massive, clean lines of the bridges dominate the pictures. In the picture of Ouse Bridge, 1800, 'a sombre power is conveyed by subordinating details to the basic tension of horizontal bridge and vertical buildings; the human activity which subtly enlivens the scene is confined to a central band parallel to the bridge' (Morris 1986, 22). In addition to the bridge, Girtin painted two other river views of York: the Ouse near Marygate, c.1797, and the New Walk, c.1798. By 1801 he was ill with a pulmonary complaint. Although his career was brutally short, he had a great influence on other artists including Varley, Linnel, Mulready and Cotman; Turner, his contemporary, described him as 'a brilliant fellow' and in a letter said 'if Tom Girtin had lived, I should have starved'.

Greig, John, fl. 1807–19

Landscape painter and lithographer who was working between 1807 and 1819. He produced a series of prints of Yorkshire antiquities from his own drawings, and in 1817 an engraving of St William's Chapel.

Grignion, Charles, 1716–1810

An important engraver, born and worked in London. Worked for many well-known 18th-century British artists, including Hogarth.

Halfpenny, Joseph, 1748–1811

Topographical artist and engraver, born in Bishopthorpe, son of the Archbishop's gardener. Trained as a house-painter, he later became an art teacher; he also painted some scenery for the Theatre Royal. Freeman of the city 1770. In 1791 and 1792 he travelled in the Lake District and Yorkshire Dales, producing attractive watercolours. He was Clerk of Works to John Carr when the latter was restoring the Minster, and repaired some of the decoration. From scaffolding he drew and in 1795–1800 published *Gothic Ornaments in the Cathedral Church of York*, reprinted 1807, 2nd edition 1831. His *Fragmenta Vetusta* (1807) contains 35 views of York buildings. Halfpenny's engravings are clear and detailed, but somewhat stiff in execution; for the most part he recorded accurately, though he was happy to omit any part of a scene he considered irrelevant to his purpose, and occasionally sacrificed accuracy in favour of clarity.

Hall, William Patrick, 1906–92

Born in York and trained at York School of Art. Moved to London 1946, then to Kent. Specialised in landscape, town scenes and architectural subjects.

Howlett, Bartholomew, 1767–1827

Engraver and draughtsman. His work was mainly antiquarian and topographical, including an engraving of Ouse Bridge in 1805. He also drew c.1,000 seals of English religious houses.

Jefferson, J. England

Architect. Studied at York School of Art. Produced sepia etchings to illustrate *Picturesque York* (1886), produced with George Benson. Ultimately settled at Whitechapel.

Jones, George Fowler, 1819–1905

Architect, born in Aberdeen, established in York in 1846. Took many photographs; those surviving comprise 64 negatives of York and 60 prints of other parts of Britain. Another 25 were used in the 1905 exhibition 'Old York Views and Worthies' in the City Art Gallery. Three were traced by his son G.H.F. Jones for inclusion in his book *Sketches in York*, 1878. For a list of G.F. Jones's photographs of York see Murray 1986, 68–9.

Le Keux, J.H., 1783–1846

Engraver, born in London. Produced work for McQueen's, fine art printers in Tottenham Court Road, London, and for other publishers, e.g. John Britton.

Lodge, William, 1649–89

Amateur artist, born in Leeds, educated at Cambridge and Lincoln's Inn, then moved to York, becoming a friend of Francis Place and a member of the 'Virtuosi'. He produced several views of York, most notably the South-West Prospect from the Mount, c.1678. Worked closely with Place on drawings and engravings, and their work is often very similar. Buried at Harewood church.

Marlow, William, 1740–1813

Born in Southwark and was a pupil with a topographical and marine painter in his early years. Studied and made copies of Canaletto's paintings, and some of his own topographical views reveal his debt to the Venetian artist. A letter of 1771 from Horace Walpole records that two views of Verona by Marlow were mistakenly sold as Canaletto's! He toured Britain in search of subjects and was Vice President of the Incorporated Society of Artists from 1778. He exhibited at the Royal Academy 1788–1807. His achievement as a topographical artist lies in his technical versatility, his balanced sense of composition, his sensitivity to lighting effects and his smooth handling of oil paint. Died in Twickenham.

Monamy, Peter, 1681–1749

Prolific marine painter, born in London. His name appears as the artist on a print of the South-West View of York in Drake's *Eboracum* of 1736, but there is no evidence that Monamy visited York to make the sketch on which the print was based. Drake may have sent him a rough sketch to work up. The print, which was folded for inclusion in *Eboracum*, would also have been sold separately.

Munn, Paul Sandby, 1773–1845

Topographical watercolour painter, born in Greenwich. Artist Paul Sandby was his godfather and probably taught him to draw. By 1799 Munn was exhibiting landscapes at the Royal Academy and 1802–13 eight of his drawings were used by the publisher John Britton (q.v.) in *The Beauties of England and Wales*. Friend of John Sell Cotman (q.v.); they made sketching tours together, including one to Yorkshire in 1803. His subjects are mostly topographical and often in pencil and monochrome wash. Exhibited work with the Old Watercolour Society. Settled at Hastings as a drawing master.

Nattes, John Claude, c.1765–1822

Draughtsman, teacher, possibly art dealer. Travelled in Italy, France and Scotland. One of the founders of the Old Watercolour Society, but expelled in 1807 for exhibiting works of others under his own name. However, his drawings of York c.1800 are probably genuine.

Nicholson, George, 1787–1878

Born in Malton. His father, George, and uncle, Francis Nicholson, were also artists. Travelled widely and produced watercolours, etchings and drawings, mainly of topographical views. His views of York date mainly from 1806–c.1840. His sketchbooks, now in York City Art Gallery, contain valuable scenes not found elsewhere, and though he occasionally varied the detail in different sketches of the same view, he is generally noted for his accuracy (Hughes 1978). Although Nicholson's artistic output was substantial, he exhibited only four works at the Royal Academy, in 1831–2.

Place, Francis, 1647–1728

Son of a country gentleman in Dinsdale, Co. Durham. Trained as a lawyer in London and later worked with the etcher Wenceslaus Hollar, who had a great influence on him. Amateur artist of considerable ability, producing topographical drawings, 'prospects', watercolours, engravings; experimented with mezzotint and with stoneware pottery. Settled in York in 1675 and from 1692 lived at the King's Manor, where he set up his own printing equipment. Became a member of the York 'Virtuosi'. Took his friend William Lodge (q.v.) on exhausting walking, fishing and painting expeditions, leading to both being arrested (quite unjustly) for suspicious behaviour during the panic over the 'Popish Plot' in 1678. Place's work provides the most important pictorial evidence for the topography of York in the late 17th and early 18th centuries. See Hake 1921; Tyler 1971.

Prout, John Skinner, 1806–76

Watercolour painter, specialising in landscapes and architectural subjects. Born in Plymouth, nephew of Samuel Prout. He was largely self-taught. His lithographs, *Antiquities of York*, were published in 1840. Travelled in Australia, Britain and France, then settled in Bristol.

Pumphrey, William, 1817–1905

Born in Worcester. Became science master at Bootham School, York, 1845. In 1849 he opened a photographic portrait gallery in Coney Street, and in 1853 published *Photographic Views of York and its Environs* (60 views). Other photographs exist, notably the south-west window of the Guildhall, the only record of the 1682 window by Henry Gyles, replaced in 1863. For a list of his photographs see Murray 1986, 23.

Ridsdale Tate, Edwin, 1862–1922

Architect and artist, with an interest in history and archaeology. Worked for Gould and Fisher, then in London and Carlisle before returning to York. Built the Tempest Anderson Hall (1912) and the Anchorage at All Saints North Street (1910). Undertook excavations at St Mary's Abbey with W.H. Brook (1912). Many drawings for guidebooks and other sketches. His historical reconstructions of early scenes in York are of considerable interest despite inevitable inaccuracies.

Rushbury, Sir Henry George, 1889–1968

Important watercolourist and etcher of architectural subjects. Studied at Birmingham College of Art. In 1912 moved to London and began to specialise in black and white prints of architectural and topographical subjects. Member of Royal Academy in 1936. Official War Artist during both World Wars, and knighted in 1964. He was very interested in York and worked in the city during three periods of his career — c.1933, in the 1940s and in 1965.

Shee, Martin Archer, 1769–1850

Portrait painter, born in Dublin. Went to London in 1788, entered as a student in the Royal Academy in 1790. Associate of the Royal Academy in 1798, full Academician by 1800. Successful portrait painter, his sitters drawn from the royal family and every rank of society. During the first half of his life his fame was overshadowed by that of his more brilliant rival, Sir Thomas Lawrence, but his portraits (including one of the York architect, Peter Atkinson, c.1820) are impressive none the less. In 1830 he became president of the Royal Academy and was knighted soon after.

Skinner, Revd J.

In 1825 he made a sketch, with notes, of a carved stone from St William's Chapel, now in the Yorkshire Museum (Flight into Egypt).

Southall, Joseph Edward, 1861–1944

Leading member of the Birmingham group of artist/craftsmen. Educated in part at Bootham School in York where he was taught watercolour by the local artist Edwin Moore. After a trip to Italy he became in 1900 co-founder of the Society of Painters in Tempera.

Talbot, W.H. Fox, 1800–77

Pioneer photographer, born in Melbury, Dorset; lived at Lacock Abbey, Wiltshire, from 1827. Visited York in July 1845. The 24 surviving negatives, now in the Science Museum, form the earliest series of photographic views of the city (listed in Murray 1986, 10).

Taylor, Thomas, c.1770–?1826

Topographical draughtsman, pupil of John Wyatt, entered the Royal Academy Schools in 1791. Exhibited at the Academy 1792–1809. Settled in Yorkshire and became an architect, responsible for a number of churches and public buildings in Leeds and the West Riding.

Toms, William Henry, d. 1765

London engraver of maps and topographical prints. Worked for antiquaries such as Sir William Stukely, and also produced many plates for Drake's *Eboracum*. Toms ran a successful engraving business for over 30 years and in 1736 produced a south-west view of the City of York.

Turner, Joseph Mallord William, 1775–1851

Born in London, he first trained with an architectural draughtsman, then entered the Royal Academy Schools at the age of fourteen. He was precociously gifted, first exhibiting a watercolour at the Royal Academy when he was only fifteen, and in 1802 he became the youngest ever full Academician. He dominated British landscape painting throughout the first half of the 19th century. From 1791 he began making regular sketching tours, in both Britain and on the Continent, later selling his drawings to engravers or working them up into watercolours. His work was inspired by history and literature as well as by nature. From the 1830s his painting became increasingly free, with detail subordinated to the general effects of colour and light.

Varley, John, 1778–1842

Artist and amateur astrologer, born in Hackney. His father was not keen on John becoming an artist, arguing that 'limning or drawing is a bad trade'. He was patronised by Dr Thomas Monro and also Edward Lascelles, for whom he was commissioned to make drawings of Harewood House. His watercolours were highly regarded and he was an influential teacher. Visited York in 1803 while on a sketching tour of Yorkshire and used material from sketches to produce later paintings. His output was prolific: the 700 watercolours he exhibited at the Old Watercolour Society between 1805 and 1842 probably comprised less than one-tenth of his total production. He produced many views of Ouse Bridge, along with other river-based sketches and paintings of York, and views of the Minster and the porch of St Margaret's Church.

Varrall, John Charles, fl. 1818–58

Line engraver who started work just before the demand for large numbers of impressions encouraged engravers to use steel rather than copper plates. Little is known of his life, but his work can be seen in many books with topographical plates.

White, Thomas

Watercolour painter and art teacher, specialising in topographical views. In York c.1800/1802. Thirty-six of his works are in the Hailstone Collection, York Minster Library. In 1802 he produced an oil painting of Ouse Bridge from the south-east.

White, Dr William

A York doctor who lived in Castlegate and kept a diary from 1 January 1782 until 1785, although entries are sporadic. It included sketch plans of parts of York (presumably those coverd by his medical practice), with each house or shop individually identified. His plans of Ouse Bridge, High and Low Ousegate, Pavement and Castlegate, with sections of adjoining streets, provide a rare glimpse of the range of shops trading in York in the late 18th century.

Whittock, Nathaniel, 1791–1860

Born in London, worked in Oxford 1824–9, then in London. He produced many lithographs, notably illustrations for Thomas Allen's topographical work on Yorkshire, 1828–31, and drew 'Bird's Eye View of the City of York' (1856, lithograph 1858).

Sources

Borthwick Institute

Faculty Papers contain many architects' plans, elevations and measured drawings. Document research by appointment. Borthwick Institute of Historical Research, St Anthony's Hall, Peasholme Green, York, YO1 7PW. Tel. 01904 642315.

Evelyn Collection, YAYAS

Glass slides and negatives of locations in York, including copies of prints and drawings mainly from originals now in York City Art Gallery, and photographs c.1900–35, with later additions, deposited in York Minster Library by the Yorkshire Architectural and York Archaeological Society. Subject index and catalogue with fuller details and contact prints of those which have been transferred to 35mm film (some 70% of the total). Permission to view from the Keeper of the Evelyn Collection, Mr S. Heppell, 56 Deramore Drive, Badger Hill, York, YO1 5HL. Tel. 01904 411224. Access by appointment with the Archivist, York Minster Library, Dean's Park, York, YO1 7JQ. Tel. 01904 611118. General enquiries 01904 625308. The Library is closed on Friday afternoons.

Mansion House

Fine collection of oil paintings and watercolours of York views. Viewing by appointment (contact the Civic Secretary). Mansion House, York, YO1 9QL. Tel. 01904 552012.

Merchant Adventurers' Hall

Watercolours, oil paintings, prints and drawings of York views, many on display in the Hall. Merchant Adventurers' Hall, Fossgate, York, YO1 9XD. Tel. 01904 654818.

RCHM

Photographs, some original, some copies of old prints and drawings, with notes, taken by the Royal Commission on the Historical Monuments of England. Filed at the National Monuments Record Centre, Kemble Drive, Swindon, SN2 2GZ. Tel. 01793 414600. General information on listed buildings available from the Listed Buildings Information Service, tel. 0207 208 8221.

Wakefield Art Gallery

The Gott Collection contains prints, drawings and wash drawings of York views produced between 1736 and 1828, notably those by Edward Abbot. Wakefield Art Gallery, Wentworth Terrace, Wakefield, West Yorkshire, WF1 3QW. Tel. 01924 305796.

West Yorkshire Archive Service

Houses the Healaugh Estate Papers (HE/50) which contain documents concerning proposals for a new Ouse Bridge in York, 1810–15, including plans. Leeds District Archives , Chapeltown Road, Sheepscar, Leeds, LS7 3AP. Tel. 0113 2145814.

YAT Collection

Photographs of maps, plans and topographical views, mainly from the RCHM collection with later additions. Catalogue, arranged topographically, in the Trust library. York Archaeological Trust for Excavation and Research Ltd, Cromwell House, 13 Ogleforth, York, YO1 7FG. Tel. 01904 663000.

York City Art Gallery

The Print Room contains the Evelyn Collection of topographical views, with many later additions. Prints and drawings are filed topographically, paintings under the artist. Viewing by appointment. York City Art Gallery, Exhibition Square, York, YO1 7EW. Tel. 01904 551861.

York Minster Library

Maps and plans, architectural drawings (York Minster), prints and drawings, photographs, 18th- and early 19th-century newspapers, together with printed books, archives and antiquarian notes relating to local history. Access by appointment with the Archivist, York Minster Library, Dean's Park, York, YO1 7JQ. Tel. 01904 611118. General enquiries 01904 625308. The Library is closed on Friday afternoons.

York Public Library: Reference Library and York History Room

Books of prints (see Bibliography, pp.111–13); folios of sketches, maps, plans, collections of old photographs. Central Library, Museum Street, York, YO1 7DS. Tel. 01904 655631.

The above information is correct at the time of publication.

For further information on collections outside York see Barley 1974.

Abbreviations

Most abbreviations are those recommended by the Council for British Archaeology, but the following are used in addition. Other abbreviations used in bibliographic references in the text are explained in the Bibliography below.

RCHM   Royal Commission on Historical Monuments
SS   Surtees Society
WYAS   West Yorkshire Archive Service
YASRS   Yorkshire Archaeological Society Record Series
YAT   York Archaeological Trust
YAYAS   Yorkshire Architectural and York Archaeological Society
YCA   York City Archive
YPSAR   *Yorkshire Philosophical Society Annual Report*

Bibliography

Manuscripts consulted

Leeds District Archives (WYAS), Healaugh Estate Papers HE/50

YCA, *YCHB*. York Corporation House Books

White, William, 1782. Plans of the Streets in York as they Appeared in January 1782 (York Reference Library)

Printed works (* = published on YAT's website)

Alexander, J. and Binski, P. (eds), 1987. *Age of Chivalry. Art in Plantagenet England 1200–1400* (London)

Attreed, L.C., 1991. *York House Books 1461–1490*, 2 vols (Stroud)

Auden, G.A. (ed.), 1906. *A Handbook to York and District, prepared for the 75th meeting of the British Association for the Advancement of Science* (York)

AY. Addyman, P.V. (ed.). *The Archaeology of York* (London)

1 D.W. Rollason with D. Gore and G. Fellows-Jensen, 1998. *Sources for York History to AD 1100*

2 *Historical Sources for York Archaeology after AD 1100:*

  2 P.M. Stell, 2002. *York Bridgemasters' Accounts**

6 *Roman Extra-mural Settlement and Roads:*

  1 D. Brinklow, R.A. Hall, J.R. Magilton and S. Donaghey, 1986. *Coney Street, Aldwark and Clementhorpe, Minor Sites, and Roman Roads*

7 *Anglian York (AD 410–876):*

  1 R.L. Kemp, 1996. *Anglian Settlement at 46–54 Fishergate*

  2 D. Tweddle, J. Moulden and E. Logan, 1999. *Anglian York: A Survey of the Evidence*

10 *The Medieval Walled City North-east of the Ouse:*

  5 J.D. Richards, 2001. *The Vicars Choral of York Minster: The College at Bedern*

11 *The Medieval Defences and Suburbs:*

  1 J.D. Richards, C. Heighway and S. Donaghey, 1989. *Union Terrace: Excavations in the Horsefair*

14 *The Past Environment of York:*

  2 H.K. Kenward and D. Williams, 1979. *Biological Evidence from the Roman Warehouses in Coney Street*

17 *The Small Finds:*

  12 A. MacGregor, A.J. Mainman and N.S.H. Rogers, 1999. *Craft, Industry and Everyday Life: Bone, Antler, Ivory and Horn form Anglo-Scandinavian and Medieval York*

  15 P.J. Ottaway and N.S.H. Rogers, 2002. *Craft, Industry and Everyday Life: Finds from Medieval York*

AY Supplementary Series:

  Wilson, B.M. and Mee, F.P., 1998. *The Medieval Parish Churches of York: The Pictorial Evidence*

Barley, M.W., 1974. *A Guide to British Topographical Collections* (London)

Benson, G., 1919. *Later Medieval York: the City and County of the City of York from 1100 to 1603* (York)

—— 1925. *York from 1603–1925*

Benson, G. and Jefferson, J.E., 1886. *Picturesque York* (York)

Besse, J., 1753. *Sufferings of Early Quakers in Yorkshire 1252–1690* (facsimile of part of the 1753 edition with introduction and index by Michael Gandy, York, 1998)

Bigland, J., 1805. *The Beauties of England and Wales*

Blair, J. and Ramsay, N., 1991. *English Medieval Industries* (London)

Bradley, T., 1891. *Yorkshire Rivers: The Ouse* (offprint from *Yorkshire Weekly Post*) (Ilkley)

Brayley, E.W., n.d. *The Works of the late Edward Dayes*

Britton, J., 1828. *Picturesque Antiquities of English Cities* (London)

Brown, H. and Brown, W., 1836. *Views of York*

Browne, J., 1847. *The History of the Metropolitan Church of St Peter, York; illustrated by extracts from authentic records, by plans, sections and engravings of architectural and sculptural details*, 2 vols (London and Oxford)

Brunskill, E., 1960. *Some York Almshouses*, York Georgian Society Occasional Paper **7**, 7

Butler, R.M., 1978. 'Views of York, 1650–1845', *York Historian* **2**, 31–42

Buttery, D., 1984. *The Vanished Buildings of York*

Caine, C. (ed.), 1897. *Analecta Eboracensia by Thomas Widdrington* (London)

Cave, H., 1813. *Antiquities of York* (London)

Clarke, M., 1976. 'Farington's "Ouse Bridge" Rediscovered', *Leeds Art Calendar* **78**, 12–15

Collins, F. (ed), 1897, 1900. *Register of the Freemen of the City of York: from the City Records* (2 vols), SS **96**, **102**

Cook, M., 1998. *Medieval Bridges* (Princes Risborough)

Cooper, T.P., 1911. *The Caves of York*

Coppack, G., 1993. *Fountains Abbey* (London)

Craster, H.H.E. and Thornton, M.E. (eds), 1934. *The Chronicle of St Mary's Abbey, York. From Bodley MS 39*, SS **148** (Durham, London)

Croft-Murray, E. and Hulton, P., 1960. *Catalogue of British Drawings, Vol.I, 16th to 17th century* (British Museum, London)

Curr, G.G., 1984. 'Who Saved York Walls? The Roles of William Etty and the Corporation of York', *York Historian* **5**, 25–38

Davidson, C. and O'Connor, D.E., 1978. *York Art: A Subject List of Extant and Lost Art, including Items Relevant to Early Drama* (Michigan)

Davies, R., 1880. *Walks Through the City of York*

Davis, V., 1985. 'The Rule of St Paul the first hermit', *Studies in Church History* **22**, 203–14

Dayes, E., 1805. *The Works of the late Edward Dayes: Containing an Excursion through the Principal Parts of Yorkshire and Derbyshire, with illustrative notes by E.W. Brayley*

—— 1825. *A Picturesque Tour through the Principal Parts of Yorkshire and Derbyshire by the late Edward Dayes, with illustrative notes by E.W. Brayley*

Dobson, R.B. (ed.), 1980. *York City Chamberlains' Account Rolls 1396–1500*, SS **192** (York)

—— 1992. 'Citizens and chantries in late medieval York' in D. Abulafia, M. Franklin and M. Rubin (eds), *Church and City 1000–1500: Essays in honour of Christopher Brooke* (Cambridge), 311–32

—— 1996. *The Jews of Medieval York and the Massacre of March 1190*, Borthwick Paper **45**, 2nd edn (York)

Drake, F., 1736. *Eboracum; or the History and Antiquities of the City of York* (London)

Duckham, B.F., 1967. *The Yorkshire Ouse. The History of a River Navigation* (Newton Abbot)

Duffy, E., 1992. *The Stripping of the Altars: Traditional Religion in England, c.1400–c.1580* (London)

Ellis, T., 1982. *The Sailing Barges of Maritime England: The Little Ships of our Canals, Rivers and Coasts*

French, T.W., 1999. *York Minster: The St William Window*, Corpus Vitrearum Medii Aevi Great Britain (Oxford)

Girouard, M., 1990. *The English Town* (Yale University Press)

Graham-Campbell, J., 1980. *The Viking World* (London)

Hake, H.H., 1921. *Some Contemporary Records relating to Francis Place, Engraver and Draughtsman, with a Catalogue of his Engraved Work*, Walpole Society Pub. **10**

Halfpenny, J., 1807. *Fragmenta Vetusta, or the Remains of Ancient Buildings in York* (York)

Hall, R.A., 1994. *Viking Age York* (London)

—— 1996. *York* (London)

Hargrove, W., 1818. *History and Description of the Ancient City of York* (2 vols) (York)

Harrison, D.F., 1992. 'Bridges and economic development, 1300–1800', *Economic History Review* **45**, 240–61

Hill, D., 1996. *Turner in the North. A Tour through Derbyshire, Yorkshire, Durham, Northumberland, the Scottish Borders, the Lake District, Lancashire and Lincolnshire in the Year 1797* (New Haven and London)

—— 1999. *Thomas Girtin, Genius in the North* (Harewood House Trust)

Hughes, J., 1978. *The Nicholson Family*, York City Art Gallery

Hutchinson, J. and Palliser, D., 1980. *York* (Edinburgh)

Interim: Archaeology in York (bulletin of The York Archaeological Trust; cited in the text as, for example, **12**/1, vol.12, part 1)

Jardine, L. 1999. *Ingenious Pursuits: Building the Scientific Revolution* (London)

Kaner, J., 1988. 'Clifton and Medieval Woolhouses', *York Historian* **8**, 2–10

Keep, H., c.1680. *Monumenta Eboracensia*, Trinity College, Cambridge (ref. 0.4.33)

Kightly, C. and Semlyen, R., 1980. *Lords of the City: the Lord Mayors of York and their Mansion House* (York)

Kitson, S., 1937. *The Life of John Sell Cotman*

Knight, C.B., 1944. *A History of the City of York* (York)

—— 1951. *This is York*

Lapidge, M., Blair, J., Keynes, S. and Scragg, D. (eds), 1999. *The Blackwell Encyclopaedia of Anglo-Saxon England* (Oxford)

Law, B., 1989. *The City of York 1886–1956*

Maor, E., 1994. *e: The Story of a Number* (Princeton)

Morris, J. (ed.), 1872–7. *Troubles of our Catholic Forefathers, Related by Themselves* (3 vols) (London)

Morris, R.K., 1989. *Churches in the Landscape*

Morris, S., 1986. *Thomas Girtin 1775–1802* (Yale Center for British Art, New Haven)

Murray, H., 1986. *Photographs and Photographers of York: the Early Years 1844–79* (YAYAS, York)

—— 1988. *Nathaniel Whittock's Bird's-Eye View of the City of York in the 1850s* (York)

—— 1997. *Scarborough, York and Leeds: The Town Plans of John Cossins 1697–1743* (York)

—— 2000. *Where to go in York: the History of Public Conveniences in York*

Murray, H., Riddick, S. and Green, R., 1990. *York Through the Eyes of the Artist* (York)

O'Connor, C., 1993. *Roman Bridges* (Cambridge)

Old York Views, 1905. *Handbook to the Old York Views and Worthies Exhibition* (York City Art Gallery)

Ottaway, P.J., 1993. *Roman York* (London)

Overman, M., 1975. *Man the Bridgebuilder* (London)

Palliser, D.M., 1978. 'The Medieval Street Names of York', *York Historian* **2**, 2–16

—— 1979. *Tudor York* (Oxford)

Palliser, D.M. and Palliser, B.M., 1979. *York As They Saw It: From Alcuin to Lord Esher* (York)

Pevsner, N., 1959. *The Buildings of England. Yorkshire: the West Riding* (Harmondsworth)

Pevsner, N. and Neave, D., 1995. *The Buildings of England. Yorkshire: York and the East Riding* (Harmondsworth)

Prout, J.S., 1840. *Antiquities of York*

Pumphrey, W., 1853. *Photographic Views of York and its Environs* (York)

Raine, A., 1955. *Mediaeval York: a Topographical Survey Based on Original Sources* (London)

Raine, J. (ed.), 1872. Register of Walter Gray, Lord Archbishop of York, SS **56**

—— (ed.), 1886. *The Historians of the Church of York and its Archbishops*

—— (ed.), 1894–5. *Yorkshire Chantry Surveys*, 2 vols, SS **91** and **92**

Rajnai, M. and Allthorpe-Guyton, M., 1979. *John Sell Cotman 1782–1842: Early Drawings (1798–1812) in Norwich Castle Museum*

RCHMY. Royal Commission on Historical Monuments (England). *An Inventory of the Historical Monuments in the City of York*. **1**: *Eburacum, Roman York* (1962); **2**: *The Defences* (1972); **3**: South-West of the Ouse (1972); **5**: *The Central Area* (1981) (HMSO, London)

Rees Jones, S., 1987. (unpublished) *Property Tenure and Rents: Some Aspects of the Topography and Economy of Medieval York*, 2 vols, PhD thesis, University of York

Ryder, P.F., 1982. *Medieval Buildings of Yorkshire* (Ashbourne)

Scott, D., 1991. *Quakerism in York 1650–1720*, Borthwick Paper **80**

Sellers, M. (ed.), 1906. *Acts and Ordinances of the Eastland Company*, Camden Soc. 3rd series **11**

—— 1918. *The York Mercers and Merchant Adventurers 1356–1917*, SS **129**

Sessions, W.K. and Sessions, E.M., 1971. *The Tukes of York in the 17th, 18th and 19th Centuries* (London)

Stell, P.M. and Hawkyard, A., 1996. 'The Lay Subsidy of 1334 for York', *York Historian* **13**, 2–14

Stow, J. 1603. *A Survey of London* (ed. C.L. Kingsford) (Oxford)

Taylor, W.B., 1990. 'The Rise and Decline of the Wholesale Butter Trade of York in the Eighteenth Century', *York Historian* **9**, 27–35

—— 1992. 'The Workshops and Manufactories of York in the Second Half of the 18th Century', *York Historian* **10**, 18–30

Torr, J., 1719. *The Antiquities of York City and the Civil Government thereof . . . collected from the Papers of Christopher Hildyard Esq.* (York)

Toy, J., 1985. *A Guide and Index to the Windows of York Minster* (York)

Tyler, R., 1971. *Francis Place, 1647–1728* (York)

VCHY. Tillot, P.M. (ed.), 1961. *The Victoria History of the Counties of England: A History of Yorkshire, The City of York* (London)

Watson, B., 1999. 'Living and Working on English Medieval Bridges' in *Medieval Life* **11**

Watson, B., Brigham, T. and Dyson, T., 2001. *London Bridge: 2000 Years of a River Crossing*, MoLAS monogr. **8** (London)

White, E. (ed.), 2000. *Feeding a City: York. The Provision of Food from Roman Times to the Beginning of the Twentieth Century* (Totnes)

Willis, R., 1973. *York As It Was*

Willmot, G.F., 1957. 'A Discovery at York', *The Museums Journal* **57**, no.2

Wilson, B.M., 1967. (unpublished) *The Corporation of York 1580–1660*, MPhil thesis, University of York

Wilson, C., 1977. *The Shrines of St William of York* (York)

Yates, N. and Gibson, J.M. (eds), 1994. *Traffic and Politics: The Construction and Management of Rochester Bridge AD 43–1993* (Woodbridge)

YAT 1988. *The Waterfronts of York: Prospects for Archaeological Research* (York)

YAT 1999. *2000 Years of York: The Archaeological Story* (York)

YCR. Raine, A. (ed.), 1946. *York Civic Records*, YASRS

YMB. Sellers, M. (ed.), 1912, 1915. *York Memorandum Book* 1, 2, SS **120**, **125**